ENTERING
THE JOB
MARKET

ENTERING THE JOB MARKET

A College Graduate's Guide to Job Hunting

MARIAN FAUX

MONARCH
PRESS

MONARCH PRESS · New York

CONTENTS

FOREWORD

My editor, Valerie Levy, first suggested that I write a book that would help new graduates get their first jobs in the real world. She noted that a book like this would also be a great service to those who hire new graduates.

Alerted to the fact that new graduates might need help job hunting, I talked to other employers—particularly those who hired college graduates right out of school. I heard the same story from everyone. Worst of all, many employers complained about two traits no one would expect to encounter in someone looking for a job: arrogance and aggressiveness. Not a few graduates, it seemed, had unusually high and unrealistic expectations about their first jobs.

A few months into my research, a newspaper story broke that would, I realized, affect the entire tone of this book. Thomas J. Moore, a reporter for the *Chicago Sun-Times*, wrote a series, which he based largely on computer research, about the employment picture for college graduates during the 1980s. He had learned that the employment picture was, in a word, bleak, at least for those who hoped and expected to use their college educations in their work. It seems that there are now twice as many college graduates as there are jobs for them.

This information meant that my book would have to take a different tack—a more direct and hard-hitting one than I had originally planned. It wouldn't suffice to write a fairly standard book about getting jobs for a generation that was going to encounter unusual difficulties in the job market. I must admit that I was not surprised to learn about the job gap. From my conversations with new graduates, I had realized that the Class of '83 already knew about it. They were in deep trouble trying to find jobs. Many were accepting jobs that did not require a college education, as some employers eagerly upgraded positions formerly filled by high school graduates. Other new graduates, some of whom were supporting themselves with part-time and temporary jobs of little interest to them, were still looking for their first real job in November, January, and even early spring after graduation.

Despite this pessimistic picture, as I continued my research, I came to feel that the job scene for new graduates was not totally bleak. I believed that those who would take the time to organize a professional job campaign, who would assess their worth realistically, and who would persevere in an extraordinarily tight job market would be able to find a college-level job within a few months.

Many, of course, would not succeed—those who held to their unrealistically high expectations of what kind of first job they should get, those who relied only on contacts and did not seek out unusual or unexpected sources of employment, those who did not realize that the work of finding a job is itself a full-time job.

For those who are willing to work, organize, and listen to advice, however, there are entry-level jobs out there. And there are some special techniques a new graduate can use to go about getting one of them.

Hunting for a job is an adventure. You can learn a lot about yourself and about what you really want out of life. In addition, it is a cumulative experience. Everything you do to find your first job will help you find later jobs, and each time you look for a job, you will draw on your past experiences and contacts to do so. In this book, you will learn not only how to find your first real job, but also how to build a solid base for all your future job-hunting efforts. Good luck!

Marian Faux
New York City

1

Figure Out Where You're Going

You're a junior or senior in college and you've begun to think about life after college. And that raises lots of questions in your mind. Foremost among those questions are ones that relate to getting a job. What kind of job do you want? If you're at all attuned to the world around you these days, you may also be asking yourself what kind of job you can get. You're probably wondering how important your first job is. And most important, what are you going to have to do to get your first job—especially in today's tight job market? The answers to these and other questions are in this book. You will learn everything you need to know to mount a successful job campaign—even in the tough market that college graduates face today.

What's Work Like, Anyway?

But first things first. Let's talk a little bit about work and jobs and how they will fit into your life. A job is what you get after college, unless you are very rich and have the option of leading an idle life. You work all year at a job, although you usually get one to four weeks off each year for good behavior. Depending on the job you get, you will need various kinds of skills, some of which can be acquired on the job. A job should let you solve problems, communicate with your fellow human beings, and express some creativity. You will need a healthy dose of ambition to move from one job to another or from one level of responsibility to another. Opportunities abound, however, for the young and ambitious.

Work, which can be loosely defined as where you go to do your job, will play a very important role in your life. You will spend a minimum of eight hours a day at full-time work, and that is, for many people, more time than they spend with their families and friends combined. You will work for approximately forty-five years.

Since you will spend so much time at work and be so involved with your job, you will want your job to be a source of personal satisfaction for you. Personal satisfaction is what, in large part, compels someone to forge a career rather than just settle for a series of unrelated jobs. But personal satisfaction does not necessarily come with every job; sometimes, you have to look and plan for it. And to obtain job satisfaction, you have to know what you want and how to go about getting it.

To begin to shape a career, and certainly to assure yourself of some degree of personal satisfaction on your first job, you need to take certain steps as you organize your search for a job. You can begin right now, as you read this chapter, by figuring out two things: what kind of work you want to do and what kind of work you are suited to do. The two may not at first look like the same animal, but with some soul-searching, they can become the same. Ideally, you should do this self-evaluation early in your senior year of college or even in your sophomore or junior year, so you can take whatever steps you feel are necessary to prepare yourself for the job market.

What Are You Best Suited to Do?

You can get an idea of the kind of work you're interested in, as well as what you are best suited for, by examining your school courses, extracurricular activities, hobbies, and part-time and summer jobs. Begin this process of self-evaluation by listing all the courses you have taken in college (or even in high school, if you think this will help) in one column. Write down the grades you received in each course in a second column. Now circle the classes that you especially enjoyed, and then circle the classes in which you did your best work—where you got the best grades.

Compare the two columns to see where you have a good match—that is, where you enjoyed a class and did well in it.

Some areas can be immediately ruled out. If you hated math and barely made it through to the end of the semester with a passing grade, it's a safe bet you aren't interested in a career in mathematics. At other times, you'll have to do a little more thinking to decide whether or not you are interested in a particular area—to say nothing of whether or not the area is properly suited to you. Suppose you love taking art classes, but mostly because you have an image of yourself as an artist. You like what you perceive to be the artist's life. You like walking around on campus with artists, dressing like an artist. This may be it, you think. But then you take a look at your grades. They aren't bad, but they aren't great either. Let's face it, you aren't exactly one of the stars of the college art circuit. Your professors aren't telling you to start taking your portfolio around to the New York galleries on your school vacations. Now is the time to be honest with yourself. Art may not be your best bet as a career.

On the other hand, suppose your best grades have been in sociology. And now that you think about it, your favorite extracurricular activity has been the four hours a week when you work part-time at a geriatric center. What does this mean? It means that your strength—and possibly the best career area for you to explore—is somewhere in the social services professions rather than in the world of art—or math, for that matter.

Before you make any final decisions, though, go through this same process of evaluation with your extracurricular activities, your hobbies and any outside interests, and any jobs you have held. List the job or activity and then write down what you performed well at along with what you especially enjoyed doing. As was the case with your courses, a pattern will begin to emerge, and you will uncover several important clues that eventually will help you to pinpoint exactly what kind of work you want to do. For now, these patterns need only be general areas of interest.

How Realistic Are Your Job Goals?

At this stage of general self-evaluation, you should also give some thought to how realistic your job goals are. Many people without any real work experience have romantic illusions about the career they want or what work will really be like. Many of their fantasies focus on the kind of job they will be able to get right out of school. Most of the time, these romantic illusions have little to do with reality. Persisting in the desire to become a great artist, for example, when there is not much basis for such an aspiration, is little more than a way of catering to your romantic illusions. Romantic illusions do not make great careers although, ironically, it's not because you can't turn a romantic illusion into a career. As a matter of fact, you probably can. But here is the catch: You won't be very happy or satisfied if you do. Your work life will always be frustrating in ways you will have difficulty accounting for.

Other people set another kind of unrealistic career goal. These are the souls whose only ambition is to become millionaires or presidents of multinational corporations by the age of thirty. These may be fine goals, but they won't help you find a job right now.

To survive in the job market you are about to enter, you have to set your sights on a job that you can realistically hope to obtain, as well as one that will satisfy you—if only for the time being. For almost everyone, this boils down to an entry-level job of one sort or another.

What's an Entry-level Job?

An entry-level job is the kind of job that is offered to 99 9/10 percent of all new college graduates. These are often training jobs that help you learn the basic skills you need to move on to a more sophisticated job. Entry-level jobs often carry titles such as "administrative assistant," "editorial assistant," "engineering trainee," or "sales trainee." In some fields, you may have to know the jargon even to be able to identify the entry-level jobs. In advertising, for example, the job of traffic manager is often open to beginners.

Job titles frequently are not very accurate descriptions of the work, and sometimes you won't know whether a position is an entry-level job until you interview for it or talk to someone about it. Although 85 percent of all jobs are primarily advertised by word-of-mouth, most *entry-level* jobs are advertised, and to learn what's available, you need only start reading the Help Wanted columns.

Coping With a Tight Job Market

In addition to the fact that you will probably have to accept an entry-level job, another kind of reality will set in when you survey the current job market for college graduates. It is tight, perhaps as tight as it has ever been. There are several reasons for this. College graduates today are part of a baby boom, a larger-than-usual generation. Just being part of a baby boom always increases the competition for jobs, but another factor is making the market even tighter for today's college graduates. Among today's baby boom youngsters, an unusually high percentage have chosen to attend college. That means that the competition for jobs requiring a college education is particularly fierce. Thomas J. Moore, the *Chicago Sun-Times* reporter who did an in-depth analysis of what he calls the "job gap," that is, the difference between the number of college graduates and the jobs requiring college skills, noted that there are now twice as many college graduates as there are suitable jobs for them. What this means is that today's college graduates not only will have to scramble hard to get a job, but they will also have to scramble hard to get a job in which they can use their college educations. For many college graduates, that is the dividing line between a job that offers satisfaction and one that does not.

But what does this all mean to you personally? How tough you will find the job market of the 1980s will depend, in part, on what you studied and where you went to school, although with twice as many college graduates as there are jobs, even a prestigious alma mater may not carry the weight it once did.

The biggest favor you can do yourself in this kind of job market—which, incidentally, is expected to continue throughout the 1980s—is to make some extra preparations to deal with the job gap. If you are a sophomore or junior reading this book, you may have time to reevaluate your major and switch to an area where the demand for jobs is especially high. If you're a senior, you may want to enroll in some practical courses the last semester of your senior year or in summer school right after your graduate. You also may have to consider some long-term actions—underemployment, for example—that will help you get the kind of job you want. Here are some specific suggestions for coping with the job market of the eighties.

Study something useful. Never mind that you've always been taught that college was the place to get a liberal arts education. Forget the old adage that you can always learn job skills on the job. In today's job market, everything counts, and recruiters are selective beyond belief. You need to arrange as many things as possible in your favor. And one of the things you might rearrange in your favor is your major area of study.

Given the job scene now and for the next few years, anyone with a technical or practical major is going to be more in demand than liberal arts majors will be. Liberal arts majors have always been at the low end of the scale in terms of employability and salary, and in the present job market the situation cannot be expected to improve. So if there is still time to change your major, beef up a practical minor, or even cram in a few practical courses, do so. (Of course, if you're not just taking liberal arts because you theoretically believe in getting a more generalized education but, in fact, because you have your heart set on teaching college philosophy somewhere, that's another matter entirely, and you will have to march to your own drummer.)

Get some basic training. Sometimes you don't have to do anything as drastic as changing your major. You simply need to add some practical courses to your curriculum. Some courses, for example, provide practical experience that can be used in any field, and they also are a signal to prospective employers that you are interested in being the best possible worker. Consider taking such practical courses as computer programming, accounting or business math, business writing, marketing and sales, typing, or basic office practices. Think about taking a few of these courses your last semester of school, or sign up for summer school at a good business college so you can tell prospective employers you're adding to your skills.

Let a vocational counselor help you decide. If you aren't sure what you want to do or what you are best suited to do, consider getting vocational counseling. Start with the career placement office at school, which may offer some testing of its own or direct you to someone who can help you.

Vocational testing is designed to help you determine where your interests and aptitudes lie. You take a series of tests, and a counselor helps to interpret the results for you.

You may ultimately have to pay for this kind of counseling, but before you do, look around for a free or inexpensive counseling service. A university or college is one of the best places to find a free clinic or service, so start making calls and asking around.

Get some work experience. The fourth thing you can do is to get some work experience. Do this through a part-time or summer job, an internship or even a volunteer position. A few years ago, any-one with a good academic record was pretty much assured of being able to get a good job. Then when the job market began to tighten up during the late seventies, recruiters got choosier, and the good jobs went to those who combined good academic records with outstanding displays of leadership in extracurricular activi-ties. Today, employers can be even more selective, and the best jobs are going to people with good academic records who have shown signs of leadership and who have also had work experience. Job experience is no longer just a sweetener in the package you offer an employer; it is a basic ingredient in many cases.

Best of all is to have some work experience in the field in which you hope to work after college. That means, basically, that you should move heaven and earth to get an internship, particularly if you want to work in a field where jobs are scarce. (The contacts you will make are as valuable as the experience.) But any work ex-perience can be turned to your favor if you handle things right during the interview. Recruiters want job candidates with some job experience because they are commonly believed to have more of an idea what is expected of them in the real world, and any work experience can provide you with insight along those lines.

The most impressive job experiences are provided by intern-ships. Give your school the first shot at placing you in an intern-ship, but if they don't have a program or you don't qualify for it, you may be able to find one through other channels. You can try approaching a prospective employer on your own and arranging your own deal, or use one of the following resources:

The Directory of Public Service Internships: Opportunities for the Graduate, Postgraduate, and Mid-Career Professional. National Society for Internships and Experimental Education, 124 St. Mary's Street, Raleigh, North Carolina 27605. (They also publish *Internships for Women.*)

1984 Internships: 16,000 On-the-Job Training Opportunities for All Types of Careers. Writer's Digest Books, 9933 Alliance Road, Cincinnati, Ohio 45245.

Consider a postcollege internship. Another way to cope with the tight job market is to plan an internship *after* you graduate. Traditionally considered a collegiate activity, internships were adapted a few years ago by women who were returning to the work force after rearing children, and today they are increasingly becoming a useful job-finding tool for college graduates who cannot break into a field any other way. Obviously, there is an important difference between an internship when you are still in college and the one you arrange after college. When you are still in college, an internship may be used to explore a career area, and there is more room for error if you find out you don't like the field after all. In a postcollege internship, you should be more sure of what you want and should even try to set up the internship with an employer for whom you would like to work full-time. Otherwise you could waste valuable time and money—yours.

Rethink Your Attitude—and Your Goals

You may find that a shift in attitude is called for before you can hope to mount a successful job campaign in today's market. More and more graduates are having to face the fact that they must settle, temporarily at least, for the kind of job that graduating seniors would not have considered a few years ago. Some new graduates are even settling for underemployment, a term that wasn't even in most college graduates' vocabularies until recently.

Underemployment involves taking a job that doesn't require that you use your college education—at least not right away. Sometimes underemployment is a trap. It can be a deep pit that you won't be able to scramble out of, but if done right, underemployment also can be a slightly more circuitous route to a job you really want and can't get at the moment. A job that underemploys you may still provide you with some basic skills, and best of all, it may offer an opportunity for advancement to a job that lets you use your education. One thing is certain: Underemployment beats unemployment by a mile.

To decide whether a particular job will underemploy you permanently (in which case you don't want it) or temporarily (meaning that it will actually open a few doors for you), you must carefully analyze and evaluate each job on its merits. Sometimes you can ask the person who interviews you what he or she thinks are the chances for advancement. Keep in mind, though, that while some employers are not at all eager to underuse their employees, others, particularly in this buyer's market, are eager to upgrade job requirements and don't flinch at shifting college graduates into dead-end jobs without acknowledging that this is what they actually are doing.

Be the Boss of Your Own Job Search

The most important way to cope with the present job market is to be in control—really on top of it. For those of you who have rather naively been leaving your futures in the hands of fate and the career placement office, new tactics may be called for. In fact, if your professors and the career placement officers at your school are still encouraging you to get a "basic" education and not worry about what you will be prepared to do after college, you have no choice but to take matters into your own hands. And that's exactly what *Entering the Job Market* is designed to help you do.

In the following chapters you will learn how to conduct a thorough and professional job search. But, in the face of an average academic record or everything you've just read about the competition, you may be feeling lost and depressed before you even start. Why bother, you ask yourself? What if you look for months and don't find anything? What if you simply can't find work you really want to do? In short, just how self-defeating is this job-hunting process going to be?

Relax. And look on the bright side. The job market isn't hopeless by a long shot, especially if you prepare yourself for what lies ahead by following the suggestions in this book. Besides, for every piece of bad news, there is usually a piece of good news to counterbalance it. So here are two things to keep in mind when you're looking for the Perfect Job:

- There may be twice as many college graduates as there are jobs, but new jobs are being created every day. Most of the jobs that exist today didn't exist fifty years ago.
- You may, in fact, get a lot of rejections as you look for a job, but you only have to get *one* acceptance to be on your way to a happy, successful career.

Also helpful to keep in mind is that even though you are a relatively inexperienced job seeker, you do have some important things to offer any employer: intelligence, eagerness to learn, willingness to tackle new areas, fresh ideas. You are, in short, new blood, and all businesses need new blood to stay alive. These qualities make you desirable—and considering that you will be paid less than a more experienced worker, they help to put you on an equal footing with some workers who have more experience or greater skills than you do.

Finally, a word of advice before you embark on your job search: Think of yourself as a professional, and act accordingly from the very first day you start looking. You don't have to be a professional to act like one, and acting like one is a very strong mark in your favor as you conduct your job search.

2

Figure Out Where the Jobs Are

Once you have begun to get some idea of where your aptitudes and interests lie—and have also developed some sense of urgency about the need to have a carefully thought out job-hunting program—the next step is to figure out where the jobs are. It's never too soon to begin thinking about job leads. Your freshman year would not have been too early, although admittedly, few freshmen concern themselves with this. By your sophomore and certainly your junior and early senior years, you should have some ideas— and at least one bulging file to back up those ideas—about the kind of work you would like to do and where you can best do it.

Keeping a General Jobs File

As soon as you get to college (or as soon as you read this, as the case may be), begin to keep a general jobs file. Into it put clippings, copies of articles, notes, brochures, annual reports, anything you can get your hands on, about industries and companies that interest you.

Items to put in this file are all around you. You may read about an interesting company in a class assignment, or a professor may use a company as a case history. Maybe you had an assignment in a computer class to trace several companies in one industry on the stock market, and you got very interested in one of them. Keep following up on that company and that industry. If you are really ambitious, try to spend an afternoon a month in a library doing general reading about careers that interest you.

Of course, you may change your mind and your major a couple of times before you settle on one field (don't throw out old files, however, in case you return to an earlier choice), but at least you will have done some homework on your future. Then, too, a company you're interested in today may have changed so radically that it no longer interests you a year or two later, but it's easier to toss out useless notes and articles than to rack your brain trying to remember which company was doing exciting research in hydraulics or which advertising company specialized in jeans accounts. Write it all down. Then file it for the day you begin a serious job search. If you are about to graduate or are already out of school and thinking about your job search, it is not too late to create a job file. Read newspapers and magazines. Take note of interesting news items or issues that appeal to you.

Beginning a Serious Job Search: The Dossier Method

When it is time to begin a serious job search—one where you find actual job leads—you will set up a more detailed filing system and undertake a larger research project.

What you are going to do is very simple, although it does involve a fair amount of work. You will develop a dossier—a file of papers containing detailed information—on each job area that interests you. In the process of building these dossiers, you will also find information on specific companies where you will eventually look for a job. These are your personal job leads.

The dossier method involves organization and research. It will require many hours of your time if you do it well, but it will pay off—in a job. Not only will your dossiers help you get a job, but they will allow you to spend less time job hunting because you will already know what you want when you start looking. They will help you impress prospective employers with your knowledge of their field and their company specifically, and it will help you beat out the competition.

Choosing a Professional Field

The very first thing you must do, if you haven't already, is to pinpoint several areas in which you think you might like to look for work. If you are very involved in your major and it, in turn, is teaching you a set of specific skills, you may already know the general area where you are likely to find work. If you aren't so sure what careers are available, make an appointment with your adviser or a career placement counselor and pick his or her brain for suggestions. You might also check out the *Occupational Outlook Handbook*, a government publication that describes jobs by occupational area and also tells the prospects of finding a job in each area.

Throughout this entire process, it helps to be a detective. You are trying to find out several important things, among them, the general areas in which you might like to work, the kind of job or jobs you are qualified to do in each area, the market value of entry-level positions, and where you will have to live if you take a job in a certain field.

Paying Attention to Geography

Certain jobs are only available in certain parts of the country. The most obvious example, of course, is the car industry. Should you

decide you want to work for a car manufacturer, you will almost
certainly have to live in Detroit at some time. California (in an
area called Silicon Valley) and Boston are considered high-tech
areas; you should consider working in one of these two places if
you work in computer technology. New Jersey is the home of
many engineering companies, and although you can probably find
work as an engineer anywhere in the country, this is one state
where you may want to focus your job-hunting efforts if you are an
engineering major. Publishers, advertising agencies, and major
public relations firms are located in large cities—New York, Los
Angeles, and Chicago, to be exact. Where you will live depends on
the profession in which you find work, and the profession in which
you find work, in turn, depends upon where you're willing to locate yourself. At this stage, you'll want to begin to pay some attention to geography, both in terms of where you want to live and
where you can get a job.

Checking Out the Market Value of Careers That Interest You

The market value of a job is what an employer will pay an employee for doing that job. Just as cars and fur coats and almost anything in our society have an agreed-upon market value, so do jobs.
The market value of a job, however, is usually not a set figure but
is, rather, a salary range. It may vary by as much as $1,000 to $6,-
000 or more at the entry level.

The market value of a job has little to do with the kind of work
that is done. It has to do with supply and demand. In a field where
there are not enough workers to fill all the jobs, even entry-level
jobs will pay well. In the so-called glamour fields—publishing,
communications, journalism—where there are more applicants
than there are jobs, the pay is generally low.

In addition to the number of people seeking work, the market
value of a job also depends on the general state of the economy.
Salaries for entry-level jobs fall during recessions and rise during
boom periods. There are also fewer entry-level jobs available dur-

ing a recession. If the predicted economic recovery continues over the next few years, it may somewhat counterbalance the glut of college graduates on the market.

There are several things you can do to research the market value of the kinds of entry-level jobs you are seeking:

- Ask other beginners, that is, persons you know who have taken jobs in the past two or three years. Most people don't want to tell anyone what they're earning, but you can ask for a range—and remind them it's not what they're earning now you're interested in, but what they earned a couple of years ago when they started out.
- Read help-wanted advertisements because they often state a salary range, particularly for entry-level jobs.
- Check ads in professional and trade association publications.
- Check government statistics, particularly those published by the Bureau of Labor Statistics. If the figures are not recent, be sure to adjust them to cover inflation.

Gathering Information: Where to Look

At the same time you are rounding up information on career areas, market value, and geographic locations, you will also find yourself uncovering information about specific companies that might want to employ you. You will have two uses for this kind of information: First, you will develop genuine job leads; and second, you will have the necessary background data you need to interview successfully with these companies.

Most of your research will be conducted through reading and in the library, although you will also spend some time talking to contacts—people who can tell you about professional areas and specific companies and jobs. There are four important resources for job information and leads: the library, which is the most important resource of all; the school career placement office; the alumni association; and employment agencies. You can expect to obtain different kinds of help from each resource. Use these resources to educate yourself (learning doesn't stop when you are handed your diploma).

The Library: The Heart of Job Research

The library is where you will do most of your valuable job research. You should start there, and you will undoubtedly return many times to check out companies where you are considering employment. The library is where you will pinpoint the fields that you will explore for employment, and where you will build up bulging dossiers on various industries and companies. Before you can put a library to work for you, you must know what it contains that will be of help to you.

Start by going, if possible, to a specialized library. First, find out if your campus has a career placement library. It may be in the career placement office, in a corner of the main library, or in a specialized library. If there is no career placement library, most specialized libraries will have extensive files that you can use for your work. If you are looking for a job in mental health, for example, head to the psychology library, the human sciences library, or the social sciences library; for a job in business, head to the business library; for one in engineering, to the engineering library. The larger your campus, the more specialized the libraries, and the more libraries there will be.

When you find the library that has the most potential for helping you, introduce yourself to a librarian and tell him or her that you are exploring fields and companies as potential sources of employment. Indicate whether you are interested in finding companies (what kind, size, etc.) or doing general or specialized reading at this stage. Armed with this information, the librarian will undoubtedly point you in the right direction to get started. Don't let your relationship with the librarian stop here, however. Once you have delved into everything that was suggested, go back and ask for still more information. If you have been reading books from the shelves, ask if there is anything you might need in the vertical files. Find out if there is a file of annual reports on companies, any newsletters that might help you, a trade publication you might have overlooked. If you and the librarian put your heads together, you won't overlook anything.

When You're Doing General Reading

When you are still exploring several career areas and trying to get a fix on one particular field, you will probably start with general reading. Regardless of the field you plan to enter, there are several publications that will help you develop an overview of the work world in general and what is going on in it these days. For general reading, try browsing through the pages of *U.S. News & World Report* (great on life-styles and trends of a statistical nature), *Time, Newsweek, Business Week, Fortune, Forbes*, the *Wall Street Journal*, the *New York Times, Barrons*, and the business pages of any newspaper in a community where you are thinking of settling or your particular profession flourishes. You are looking for—and should be taking notes on—growth industries and trends within each industry (to see where the jobs really are), promotions, key officers and employees (to get some idea of how much turnover there is in the field), size of businesses and general locations throughout the country, and the overall financial health of the industry. You should also jot down the names of companies that are mentioned specifically: You will put these to use in the next phase of your research.

Reading the Trade Press

Once you have spent a few weeks on general reading, you should be ready to move on to the trade press. The trade press consists of those periodicals, newsletters, and newspapers published specifically for individual occupations. They are for insiders, and they report on the gossip, trends, and movement of employees within the field, among other things. For example, the primary trade publication in advertising is *Advertising Age;* people who work in publishing read a magazine called *Publishers Weekly.*

You won't have much difficulty finding the trade publication in whatever field you are investigating. Here are some reference books to help you locate the pertinent publications:

> *Standard Periodical Directory*
> *The Encyclopedia of Business Information Sources*
> *Standard Rate & Data*
> *Business Periodicals Index*
> *Ayers Guide to Periodicals*

There are even specialized directories to the trade press of various occupations. For example, engineers should ask the librarian for *Engineering Index*, and industrial artists should check out the *Industrial Arts Index*, both of which will introduce you to these professions' respective trade presses. These are general reference books and the fastest way to find them is to ask the librarian where they are kept.

Investigating Individual Companies

Once you begin to build your files on individual companies, there will be still another, more specific, category of reading. While continuing all the reading that has been discussed, now look specifically for companies that might prove to be potential employers. Start by locating about twenty that interest you for one reason or another: They are leaders in their field, are innovators, have unique training programs, offer opportunities for advancement, and most basic of all, have job openings. Don't limit yourself to the giants or the leaders in the field the first time around, but instead investigate medium-sized and small businesses, too. Sometimes smaller companies offer better growth opportunities and a more flexible job structure than large companies. Too many new graduates only go for the giants when they start interviewing; this is a mistake if only because you have nothing to compare them with. Even if you think you want to work for a company of a specific size, do some comparison shopping if possible, so you have a solid basis for making your final decision of where to go to work.

Good references to use in tracking down individual companies are Dun & Bradstreet's *Million Dollar Directory* (large firms) and *Middle Market Directory*. You might also check Standard & Poor's *Register of Corporations, Directories and Executives*, and *Thomas' Register*. Reference books like these list the type, size, and scope of operations, as well as the names of top officers. For more specific information, read annual reports and check the vertical files for items relating to these companies.

A final source that is both general and specialized is the trade report issued by major consulting firms. Names to look for are the Batelle Memorial Institute; A. S. Hansen, Inc.; Hay Associates; Hewitt Associations; Organization Resources Counselors; and Cole, Warren, and Long, Inc.

Once you have developed your own files on two or three fields you would like to work in and have established twenty or so contacts in each field, you have completed your basic research. Although this sounds like a lot of work, it can be accomplished in a few hours a week in the library. Of course, the more time you spend on your research, the better equipped you will be during your job search. Ideally, you should stretch out the research over a semester or more. It eases your work load, but more important, it gives you a chance to watch trends in one or more areas over several months.

Until you do this kind of research, you will not realize how much self-confidence it will give you. It's just like the difference between studying and not studying for a tough examination. If you've done your homework, you will go into any interview very well prepared. You will know what you are looking for and how reasonable your ambitions are, and you will also be developing a clear picture of what the company is looking for and how you can best fit the bill.

The Placement Office

When your library research is well under way, it is time to avail yourself of the other major resources for finding a job. Turn next to the college placement office. You will be well prepared to work with them if you have done the library research.

Colleges and universities run placement or career counseling offices to help place their graduates in their first job. (They also offer some limited assistance with later job searches, but their help is never so intense or so concentrated as when they are trying to place graduating seniors.) Placement is something universities do only partly as a service to you, and partly to benefit themselves. Your university does, indeed, want you to find a job because you need one, but it also makes the institution look good to have employable graduates.

How they work is another matter, one that varies from school to school and even from placement officer to placement officer. One of the first things you should do is to attach yourself to a competent, ambitious counselor who acknowledges your potential and will help you find the best "fit" between you and a career field.

Placement offices go into high gear for graduating seniors about the end of their first semester. Throughout the second semester, they are very busy matching seniors to recruiting companies. But—and this is something you may not be aware of—placement offices do not necessarily match *every* senior to a job. It would be an impossible task even in the best of times, and these are not the best of times for college graduates seeking jobs. Campus recruitment by companies has declined by 40 percent in the last two years, and although it can be expected to rise somewhat as the economy recovers, the overall trend is one of decline. At one major East Coast state university, for example, with a typically active college placement office, fewer students are getting interviews these days. In the school year 1982–83, of the 116,000 requests for interviews, only about 21,000 were arranged. That is 13 percent more interviews than the year before, but since there were more students, only 20 percent of the students got any interviews at all, compared to 30 percent in the preceding year.

Since not everyone gets to interview through the placement office, who does? First, it helps to have a superb record both academically and in extracurricular activities. Second, it helps to be looking for a job in an area where there are more jobs than job seekers. Liberal arts majors often get little help at career placement offices because they are more difficult to match up with a specific industry.

Furthermore, in many college placement offices, once the interviews have been set up, you get very little in the way of counseling. Remember, too, that the placement office wants to help you get a job, almost any job, but not necessarily a great job. Getting a great job is something you do for yourself.

Still you should take advantage of every possible avenue of support when looking for a job, and that includes the placement office. If they can get you interviews, fine; take them, even though they will often be "quickies"—fifteen minute, assembly-line appointments.

You should also investigate other ways the placement office can help you. Do you have access to their files (an excellent source for your dossiers)? Do they offer any seminars on job-hunting skills? Some schools have established sophisticated services such as videotaped sessions to help you improve your interviewing skills. By all means, take advantage of anything along these lines.

Finally, use your career counselor as a source of information. Let the counselor suggest places where you can look on your own or advise you on interviewing techniques.

Even if the placement office helps you, be aware of its limitations. Certain companies only recruit at certain schools, and if your school isn't on the circuit, there is little your placement office can do to help you get an interview with a particular company. Therefore, it behooves you to check out early in the game what companies—what kind of companies—will be putting in an appearance at your school. You may find that you'll have to make contacts on your own if you want to interview with certain companies. Most schools publish a list of companies that will be recruiting on campus. Get a copy of this as soon as possible, and look it over to see how much help the placement office will be with your interviews.

Alumni and Alumnae Offices

Although alumni associations are not placement offices, they can provide some valuable contacts for job seekers not only when they have just graduated but throughout their careers. Most of the time you aren't eligible to join an alumni association until after you graduate, but if you intend to use it for job contacts, you should start attending meetings the summer you graduate. Some associations have clubs that are like restaurants, hotels, and health clubs all rolled into one; it's easy to socialize for business purposes at these places. Others only have a meeting place and may meet as infrequently as once a month. Find out when the meetings are and attend them. Be sure to tell people that you're looking for a job and what kind of job you're looking for. You've got a special tie with these people, plus—since they graduated from the same school you did—many of them could very well be working in the field in which you hope to find a job.

Trade Associations

Another important source of information about jobs is the trade association. Some have junior memberships, which means you can join while you are still in college, but you can join most after you graduate. To find out which associations are active in areas that interest you, contact the placement office or go to the library and ask to see *The Encyclopedia of Associations,* which lists over 1,200 trade associations. You can use your membership in a trade association the same way you can use your membership in an alumni association. Go to meetings, become active, and talk to lots of people about your job search. You will undoubtedly be able to drum up a few contacts through this kind of network. In addition, call the trade association office. Some associations sponsor a placement program, as well as seminars on job-hunting or even additional job training. Many have fact sheets or files about prospective employers that are open to members.

Employment Agencies

Employment agencies used to be one of the last places that college graduates turned to, but today new graduates are actively using them. Before contacting an agency, you need to know a little bit about them. Employment agencies can be either privately or publicly owned. You will probably work through a private agency if you decide to use one at all; state-owned agencies usually are geared to blue-collar and unskilled workers. Unlike the college placement office, which is rather benign and if it doesn't have your best interests at heart at least will do no real damage, employment agencies do not always have your best interests at heart, and they don't care if they do any damage as long as they can earn some money with you. Some agencies will place you—even pressure you—into any kind of job so they can get the commission. While the better ones will try to match you to the job to some extent (after all, they want repeat business from the company), they don't work very hard at this on entry-level jobs.

Employment agencies can also be rough on your ego because they will constantly remind you how limited your skills are and how you ought to be happy to get any kind of entry-level job. Depending upon the agency, the only job skill that may carry any real weight with them is the number of words per minute that you can type.

Despite this lukewarm recommendation, you should not rule out employment agencies, particularly if you have graduated and are still looking for a job. The trick to working with an agency, though, is to be sure that you use them and not the other way around.

You also need to realize that agencies will have a time limit— often as short as two weeks—and if they have not placed you within that time, they won't do much for you afterward. In a sense, this is good news. You can give up two weeks of your life to letting an agency see what it can do for you. Here are some hints on dealing with employment agencies:

- Find a good one. Basically, this means one that has bona fide jobs. If you repeatedly ask to interview for a job that you saw in the help-wanted ads and they say it is filled, begin to wonder if the job ever existed or whether it was just an advertising "come-on" for the agency. It's illegal to advertise a job that doesn't exist, but some agencies do this anyway.

- Make sure the person you work with is someone you would want contacting companies on your behalf.
- Don't work through any agency that asks you to pay the fee. Agencies get paid for the work they do— usually a percentage of the first year's salary—but the money should come from the employer and never from you. There is no law prohibiting agencies from charging the job seeker; you just don't want to get involved with one at this early stage of your career.
- Don't pay for any extras, either. You don't need vocational testing, or if you do, this isn't the place to get it. Do not sign anything that obligates you in this way.
- You will be asked to sign something, however. Read it very carefully first. You probably will promise not to contact on your own any company where you interview for a certain period of time. This shouldn't produce much conflict, assuming you have turned to an agency after you have used up all your contacts.
- Never permit an exclusive listing with an agency. In fact, if you're going to go the agency route, sign up with two or three qualified agencies, and let them compete with one another to find you a job.
- Cooperate. This may sound like strange advice after all these words of warning, but if you're going to work with an agency, then work *with* them. Ask what you can do to help. Listen to what they tell you about how to handle a specific interview. Rewrite your résumé if that's what they suggest. Be polite to the agency staff; after all, you do want them to work hard for you.

Setting Up a File System

As you begin to collect all this information, you will need some place to put it. Even if you don't have a file cabinet, files are a convenient way to store the data. Consider using hanging files to hold categories of information; one hanging file might be devoted to each job area where you are planning to look or to each industry you are exploring. In these hanging files, put individual manila or colored folders; you should have at least one folder for any specific company that interests you or is a likely employer. You should also maintain some general files, in such areas as job-hunting hints, contacts and key people, correspondence, cover letters and résumés, as well as a telephone log.

Put even the tiniest snippet of information in your files. If you talk to someone in the school career placement office, and he or she suggests that you interview with a couple of specific companies two months hence, make a note to that effect and put it in a file. A job search has a way of multiplying itself, and if you have not kept a filing system, you will wake up one morning and find that you have scraps of paper everywhere and that you no longer know where you are in the process. This can be disastrous. It is important not only to keep files, but also to keep them organized.

Another very important reason to set up orderly files right now is that you can use the same files for job hunting throughout your life. From this time on, you should consider job hunting a cumulative, if sometimes dormant, activity. In a year or two, when you are ready to look for your second job, or even ten years down the road when you are mounting a drive for an important executive position, these same files will be of enormous value to you.

3

Get Ready to Look

Now that you have decided what you want to do when you grow up and have gotten an idea of where you may be able to do it, the next step is to make preparations to mount a serious job campaign.

When Are the Best Times to Look for a Job?

You'll probably start serious interviewing during the last semester of your senior year—unfortunately, the very same time every other graduating senior is also looking for work. Although you cannot avoid looking then, it is not a particularly good time to look for a job for the simple reason that the market is flooded with new graduates. On the other hand, it is a valuable time to look because employers expect new graduates to show up then. They are prepared to hire in that particular category, if in no other.

Summer is also a slow season in many businesses, another thing you should brace yourself for. In fact, don't be surprised if your job-hunting efforts grind to a halt during August when many people take vacations and some manufacturers even close down their factories for two or three weeks. In case you are looking for a job in teaching or administration or just counting on the career placement office to help out, be aware that universities wind down and little work is done in August. Even businesses that don't officially close seem to slow down in August. Although you might want to give yourself some vacation time and August is probably the time to do it, it is not a good idea to take the entire summer off just because businesses slow down or close. Even if you don't find a job during the slow summer months, you'll get an A for effort when you tell prospective employers that you were busy looking for a job all summer. Spending the summer lounging by the pool is not a way to impress a prospective employer with your eagerness to enter the world of work.

November and December are another bad time to look for a job since people are usually concerning themselves with the holiday season and possible year-end bonuses.

Take heart, though, there are some very good times to look for a job. Early fall is an ideal season for job hunting. People return from vacations invigorated and filled with lots of new ideas— which often include adding more staff. There is considerable turnover at this time of year. People also tend to change jobs from January through early spring, which also creates openings.

As you can see, your biggest push should be the last semester of school—the months from January to June or July when employers are most likely to have openings. This is also when employers are the most geared up to hire new graduates even though the competition is sometimes fierce. And while you should not let up on your job-hunting efforts during the summer (although you may get depressed with the employment picture), you should also realize that fall will be a better season for you. The job market is livelier then.

Just as there are months that are good for job hunting, there are certain times of the week and day when you will find people more receptive to your inquiries about employment. Mondays, for example, are better than Fridays for making calls and going to interviews. Fridays, in fact, are the worst—Friday afternoon is a time to wind down and review what you've done that week rather than make calls. If possible, never schedule an interview on Friday afternoon if you can avoid doing so. People are not thinking about hiring new personnel, but are planning their weekend escape from office life.

Job Hunting Is a Full-time Job

Once you start to look for a job, do yourself a favor and treat your search as a full-time job. Get up in the morning and start working no later than eight or nine o'clock. Work until quitting time— that's five o'clock. And don't succumb to the temptation to give yourself a vacation in the middle of your search as so many people do. It's not good for your morale, no matter how discouraged you are. Besides, as you job hunt, you will build a kind of momentum which you risk losing if you take time off.

As you look for your first real job, you should work at least as hard for yourself as you would for any employer. Furthermore, keep in mind that finding your first job is one of the most important jobs you will ever undertake. It's the basis for all the other jobs you will ever have.

Supplies for the Job Hunt

Two important steps in getting ready to look for a job are to get the supplies you need to do the job right and to organize a few simple files that will help you keep track of your progress.

Several weeks before you start to contact companies for interviews, you should order some business stationery. You will definitely need paper to write letters on, and you may want to treat yourself to some business cards.

Buy the best stationery you can afford. Prices and quality, as well as printing techniques, vary, so shop around to get the best deal for your budget. If possible, the stationery should be printed with your name, address, city or town, state, zip code, and telephone number. This may not be possible if you do not yet have a permanent address, in which case just have your name printed. The paper should be business-sized, that is, 8½-by-11 inches, rather than the smaller 5-by-8-inch size, which is mostly used for social correspondence.

White is the best color for the simple reason that it cannot offend anyone. Good alternate colors, if you must, are gray or beige, but if you choose a color, be sure it coordinates with the paper on which you print your résumé. You wouldn't want gray stationery and a beige résumé, for example, nor would you even want a yellow cast to any white paper you put with gray stationery. Buy envelopes that match the stationery.

You can be a little less conservative when choosing a business card, although neither the card nor your stationery should contain a logo of any kind or a monogram. Business cards should be white or off-white if you know you will be interviewing in a field that still hews to a conservative tradition (law firms, banks, certain investment firms, for example), but in any other area you can choose a gray or beige card and a slightly more elegant or unusual typeface than you might want to use on your stationery. Get a standard-sized card—3½ by 2 inches—because that is what fits into most people's telephone files and card cases. The extra attention you get from a larger-than-usual card is offset by the chances that it will be misplaced or lost more easily than a standard-sized one.

Once you have ordered business cards, it helps to know when and how to use them. Attach your card to the top of your stationery, preferably with a paper clip rather than a staple, when you first contact someone. The letter can go into your prospective employer's file, and the card can be detached and kept in sight or put into his/her telephone file. You should also carry cards with you, so you can leave them with people whenever you are asked for your phone number. If someone even glances at your résumé during an interview and comments, "I can contact you at this number, then," pull out a card and offer it to him or her.

Organizing Your Job Search With a System

Once you are in the midst of job hunting, things may start happening rather quickly (if you're lucky). And if you haven't already set up some kind of system, you may find yourself making some wasteful mistakes, such as losing the name of the person who interviewed you four months ago and told you to contact him again, or not having an important phone number, or answering the same blind ad twice. The only way to avoid these embarrassing blunders is to set up a few simple files that will help you keep track of exactly what is going on at all times.

You can use note cards, files, or charts—whichever suits you best. If you start out using one method and realize it isn't working for you, take the time to switch. Find the system that works for *you.*

Whatever method you use, record the following information:

Name of the person contacted
Name of any other contacts (and don't overlook secretaries)
Company name
Company address and telephone number
Name of the person who gave you the job lead or referred you to the company
Date of your initial contact
Date you sent a cover letter and résumé
Date of an interview, if any
Date of any follow-up steps

If you will be contacting a lot of companies, say, more than twenty, a card system is probably your best bet because you can then write one card for every job lead or one card for every company you contact. Depending on how detailed the information is that you plan to keep, use either 3-by-5-inch or 4-by-6-inch cards. Store the cards in a metal file box with alphabetical dividers.

Another advantage of using cards is that they provide room to jot down personal impressions about job descriptions or persons who interviewed you. If your job-hunting efforts extend over several weeks or months, as they likely will, or if you anticipate talking to a lot of different people at different companies, then *don't count on your memory.* Put your impressions in writing, so you can review your initial reaction when you find yourself being offered a job by some company that may have interviewed you several months ago. The interview process is not usually so extended and as a rule, you will be in pretty steady contact with any company that is thinking of hiring you, but there are exceptions. There is, for example, the company that interviews you in June but won't have an opening until late fall, or the interviewer who doesn't offer you one job but who then recommends you for another job a few months later that is a better fit. At such times, you will want to have notes to refresh your memory.

You can also use the cards to make specific notes about what you discussed with the interviewer—including anything personal. Of course, if you discussed salary ranges, you should definitely put that in writing immediately after the interview, but you will also find it helpful in a second or third interview if you can check the card and instantly recall that the interviewer knows your second cousin in Baton Rouge; or that she talked to you a lot about her daughter, who is about to attend your alma mater; or that she studied agronomy even though she ended up in insurance.

Regardless of whatever detailed method you use to organize your job leads, you will also probably find it helpful to keep a more condensed chart that provides a ready reference to where you are in your search. A sample of this kind of chart follows.

As you look for a job, keep your files updated. Don't let them become disorganized or sloppy because you're sure you're going to have a job next week. "Next week" can, unfortunately, easily

Company	Date sent	Interview	Thank-you note sent	Follow-up comments
ABC	8/5/84	8/20/84	8/21/84	No job now; opening expected mid-Sept.
LMP	8/5/84	None	8/17/84	Check back late Sept.
XYZ	8/5/84	8/23/84	8/23/84	They will call.

stretch to three or four weeks or even several months in a job search. You will need to have your files on hand until you have accepted a job. And then you should store them and keep them for your next job search.

Putting Those All-Important Contacts to Work

A very important step in preparing to job hunt is to line up and evaluate your contacts. Contacts, more often referred to today as "connections," are probably the single most important aid in job hunting. In your first heavy-duty round, you should exhaust every possible contact for once you have done that, unfortunately, job hunting becomes a somewhat more difficult task.

Asking for a Reference

When you ask someone to give you a reference, you are asking if you can present his or her name to prospective employers as someone who can vouch for you. Ideally, a reference is someone you have worked for, but employers understand that you may never have held a job, so new graduates can also provide personal or character references. These include family friends; members of the clergy; professors with whom you have worked, although technically speaking, a professor's recommendation might be considered professional; and anyone else who knows you well enough to vouch for the fact that you will probably show up on time and not plan an after-hours robbery of the company safe. The person who recommends you must know you reasonably well in order to give you the kind of glowing reference that will make someone want to hire you, so it is worth your while to get to know your professors and anyone else who has any clout and who might be able to speak well of you.

Don't overlook the possibility of using former employers as references, even if the job you held was not directly related to the kind of work you hope to be doing. Any kind of work experience is better than none, and any kind of previous employer who will be able to make some kind of comment about your general abilities as a worker is better than a more general reference. Along the same lines, consider using anyone for whom you have done volunteer work since this person will be able to vouch for your ambition, reliability, and dependability—the traits employers seek.

Finally, when you contact potential references, let them know what kind of job you are looking for and ask them if they have any ideas about companies or persons where you might find a job. People who like you enough to give you a reference often function somewhat in the manner of godparents: They take a very special interest in you and will help out in any way they can. Use them in your network system.

Often the question arises of how well you have to know someone to request a reference. Perhaps you did a research paper for a professor who knows you quite well, but there is another professor whom you don't know well but who does a lot of consulting work in the field where you hope to work and who would, you quite correctly decide, be an excellent reference. Do you ask the person who does not know you well but carries a lot of weight?

At the risk of chiding you after the fact, this is exactly the kind of person whom you should have been cultivating all along—in part, so you could ask for the reference and be assured of getting a good one. The kind of reference you can hope to get is the entire issue. Most employers value a recommendation or reference that will aid them in the selection process. A broad, generalized recommendation that doesn't make you stand out from the rest will often not be offset by a well-known name in the field in which you're interested.

An alternative is to get to know the "star" well enough so that he will be able to recommend you honestly and accurately. Ask to meet with him to advise you on your job-hunting strategies. Your recommender will undoubtedly be flattered, and will probably be able to offer valuable insight.

Some words of caution: Don't go overboard on supplying references to a prospective employer. No one wants or needs to call more than three or four people. Once you have asked and gotten permission, type out all the names, titles, addresses, and telephone numbers on a clean sheet of typing paper, and have copies made so you can hand them to anyone who asks you to supply references.

You should never give someone as a reference without having first obtained permission. And you should ask permission each time you embark on a job hunt. This does not mean for every job, but rather, for each major search. If you even cease job hunting for several months, it is a good idea to check in with your references to let them know what you're doing and to ask for their permission (a necessary formality at this stage) to use their names once again. Actually, this little formality of checking in again can work to your advantage since it is only smart to maintain contact with your references and to keep them apprised of your progress. If you want to, and feel comfortable doing so, you can even alert a reference when you know he will be called. That gives you a chance to prime him a little, too, by describing the job and the kind of person who will be needed to fill it. To this end, you should also provide your references with copies of your résumé, along with a note reminding them that they may be called on to speak in your behalf. Whenever anyone is kind enough to give you a reference, you should always drop him or her a thank-you note. And you should send thank-you notes when you get a job.

Don't carry around letters of reference to hand out to prospective employers. They won't carry much weight, if any, since you obviously would not have these letters in your possession if they spoke of you in less than glowing terms. Unfortunately, you have to trust in powers greater than yourself, i.e., the persons whom you have chosen as references, when it comes to what they actually say about you. A sensitive person will occasionally send you a carbon copy of a reference letter he or she has written about you, but keep in mind that many references are given over the phone.

What, then, can you do if you suspect that someone is not going to give you a good reference? This problem usually arises later in your career, when you have perhaps been fired or when you have had an unpleasant experience with a former employer. It is almost unheard of for someone to give a new graduate a poor rating, but this is assuming that the new graduate chooses references very carefully.

How do you know who is likely to give you a good reference? Reputation can carry some weight. Talk to friends and former students who might have had experiences with your prospective recommender. Use your instincts. Many professors, in particular, will, in fact, decline to write the recommendation because they are too busy. It is more often wiser to select someone else than to be too pushy. Chances are this person is really too busy or is actually saving you from a mediocre reference.

Asking for Job Leads

As noted earlier, the people who give you references may also be a good source of job leads—but they shouldn't be your only source. To find job leads, you should call on every single person you know who might conceivably be of any assistance at all. Don't panic— you know lots more people than you think, hundreds of people, in fact. There are your friends, your acquaintances, your parents' friends and acquaintances, your siblings' friends and acquaintances. There are people in groups you belong to as well as all those peripheral people whom you don't consider either friends or acquaintances but whom you certainly know well enough to inform of your job-hunting efforts. It has been said that no American has to call more than three people to get in touch with the President of the United States. If that's true, then the distance between you and the job of your dreams probably is no farther than your circle of friends and acquaintances.

Then pass the word to everyone you know. Tell the family

butcher when you pick up an order; tell your parents' bridge group; visit your parents at work; chat with anyone who will listen to your plans about the future. In fact, if you have never taken time to say more than "hello" and "good-bye" to your parents' friends, now is the time to become a bit more outgoing. You certainly don't want to bore anyone with your job hunt or "attack" anyone you meet, but the more people you let in on what you are up to, the more job leads that will materialize.

One enterprising young woman, whose father wielded a great deal of power and who could easily have gotten many interviews with people he knew, instead chose a more unusual way to use this valuable set of contacts. She wrote short, personal letters to about fifty of her father's business contacts. She described her status— she was finishing school and eager to start working—and also mentioned her high academic standing and the kind of job she hoped to get. In her concluding paragraph, she asked them for any help, i.e., job leads or suggestions, they might feel they could give. She did not ask for or suggest interviews. The tone of her letter was very respectful, and she mentioned that she realized how busy these people were. When she did a few follow-up calls just to test the waters, she discovered not only that almost everyone had a job lead, but also that several people wanted to see her in person— which, of course, led to still more job leads.

This technique is very close to the kind advocated by networks. Networks, loosely organized groups of people with similar professional interests (women lawyers, executives over forty, pediatric research physicians, for example), became a red-hot idea in the late seventies. Their rise coincided, not at all coincidentally, with the growing numbers of women who were entering the work force. Many women took note of the "old boy" networks that men had naturally formed as a result of attending the same schools, belonging to the same clubs, and lunching in the same restaurants over many years.

Networking: Does It Help or Hurt?

The idea of networking also led to the development of a new job-hunting technique: The information-gathering interview, in which someone, usually with the encouragement of a network, calls up someone else, often an executive with a loose affiliation to the network, and asks if he or she would take some time to "talk." Ostensibly, this is not a job interview, but there is always the hope or possibility that a job will eventually materialize, often under the auspices of the executive who granted the purely exploratory interview.

This explanation of networks and the information-gathering interview is all by way of letting you know that this method has gotten a little stale through overuse. More and more often today, executives feel that networkers have worn out their welcome. They report that too many networkers often have only vague ideas about the kind of work they are seeking; they often have no real link to the person they seek to interview (even though they often claim they do); and they aren't especially appreciative of any help they receive. So before you align yourself with a network, or use the networker's technique of asking an executive for an information-gathering interview, you may want to weigh just how much it will help you. (Chapter 8 contains a lengthier discussion of information-gathering interviews and will help you decide whether this technique is for you.)

Cold Calls: What They Are and When to Use Them

When you have exhausted all your connections or at least done as much with them as is possible for the moment, and when you have overruled the possibility of using a networking technique, then you have one option left to round up job leads: cold calls. In sales jargon, cold calls are ones made to persons whom you do not know and with whom you have no connection. They might be names you have gotten from directories, trade associations, or through any of the sources outlined in Chapter 2. In our context, you make a cold call to find out whether a company has any job openings for which you are qualified.

The Rule of Three

Cold calls are not so scary as they sound, especially if you use what Thomas Moore calls the Rule of Three. His theory is that anyone needs three good contacts with a person before he or she becomes real—a personality rather than an anonymous voice or face. The Rule of Three means you don't have to remain a cold caller very long; in fact, the only real cold call you make is the initial one when you introduce yourself. Most of the time, you won't even have to do that in person as it's usually better to send a letter along with your résumé as your initial contact. The opportunities for putting the Rule of Three into effect in a job search are many: the initial call, sending your résumé and a cover letter, a follow-up call to ask for an interview, the interview itself, a follow-up call, a thank-you note or letter—but that's all a little farther down the road.

Once you have rounded up a sizable number of job leads, gathered both from friends and acquaintances and from cold calls, you should divide them into A, B, and C lists. On the A list put leads that are urgent and must be followed up right away, as well as those obtained through connections or ones that are unusually solid for one reason or another. On the B list put contacts you can turn to when you have finished the A list, which like all three lists will be constantly expanding and contracting as you follow up. The C list contains the least likely prospects, but it is definitely not a throwaway. Lots of people have found great jobs from their C lists, and the key to a successful job hunt is to cover all bases as thoroughly as possible.

As you can see, you have some work to do before you can even begin to job hunt. Actually, setting up is not as complicated as it seems when you first think about it. You'll probably need a week to ten days to get ready to job hunt. After that, the next step is to write a résumé—and after that, you start sending out résumés and cover letters, which will almost immediately lead to interviews. And we all know where *they* lead.

4

That All-Important Cover Letter

Have you ever wandered into a corporate headquarters or the lobby of a major office building and found one of those lobby exhibits that have become so popular? They are invariably interesting, and many are informative or even of some artistic merit, but in each case, an attempt is being made to sell you something—a product, a service, or, as is often the case, an idea or a point of view.

The process of getting ready to look for a job is a little like mounting one of those exhibits. You prepare a display, which you then use to persuade someone to adopt a point of view, namely, that you would be a useful employee. You are the product, and your goal is to persuade someone to give you an interesting job.

A typical job-hunting display basically consists of cover letters, résumés, and interviews. (The latter might be considered the audiovisual part of this display; think of it as multimedia, if you can.) In this chapter and the chapters that follow, you can explore each of these job-hunting tools in detail and discover how each one can best be put to work for you.

Only a few years ago, most of the emphasis in a job-hunting exhibit was focused on the résumé, which was considered the primary selling tool. And for several years—at about the same time, ironically, when the economy was struggling with inflation—résumés also became very inflated. Puffery, exaggeration, and outright lies became the norm and were even expected on a résumé. Today, the puffery has deflated considerably, and résumés are more straightforward and plainspeaking. Instead, cover letters have taken over as the most important item in a job hunter's bag of tricks.

Where the cover letter used to basically consist of a few short facts ("In response to your advertisement in the *Times* on Sunday, April 13, I am enclosing my résumé. Sincerely, John Doe IV"), now it is the cover letter that shows you off and the résumé that is the basic fact sheet. The cover letter, therefore, deserves equal, if not more, preparation time than the résumé. What's more, you should *never* send a résumé without also sending a cover letter.

What a Cover Letter Can Do for You

The first thing a cover letter does is introduce you. That is why you should always include a cover letter with every résumé you mail out. If a prospective employer receives your résumé with no letter attached, what is he to think of it? Do you want a job? Which job? Are you interested in his company? Do you want an interview? Are you just submitting your résumé for the job files? As you can see, an unaccompanied résumé raises more questions than it answers. The answers, however, can all be supplied in a well-written cover letter.

The second purpose of a cover letter is to point out any reasons that this job—or this company, if you are not sure what job is available—is right for you.

The third and final thing a cover letter does is to give you a forum for requesting an interview. Asking for an interview is very much like closing a sale in business. You have shown off the product, described its benefits in general, described its benefits to the person, and at this point, many inexperienced salespersons lose the sale because they forget to ask the customer to buy their product. A direct request to someone to buy something is the "closing" of a sale, and in a good cover letter, you should always "close" by asking the recipient for an interview.

The Tone of a Cover Letter

A cover letter must be something of an attention-getter. It must make the reader want to turn the page and check out your résumé. But—and this is important—it must be an acceptable kind of attention-getter. A man we'll call Joe wanted a job in publishing a few years ago. Actually, he did not want a job in publishing initially: A few years out of Yale Drama School, he wanted to be—and believed he was —the world's greatest playwright. He wanted to write, but knew he needed a job to support himself—and publishing seemed an area where he could put his skills to use. Using a friend's contact, he wrote a cover letter to a publisher at a major New York publishing house. Rather than modestly touting his skills as a potential editorial assistant and sometime proofreader, however, he offered suggestions in his letter for how the president might improve the line of books he published. Joe was full of ideas, most of which served only to point out how little he knew about publishing. Joe was also full of something else—arrogance, a trait that is, quite frankly, a little too common in college-educated but inexperienced job hunters. His letter proved to be ineffective. When you are told that a cover letter must be an attention-getter, keep in mind that this means only that it must be well thought out, organized, concise, and somewhat persuasive. It should also strike a note of humility.

A cover letter is the most personal job-hunting tool. This doesn't mean friendly, but rather, that the letter should be clearly earmarked for one special person. A cover letter—even if it is—should never look like part of a mass mailing.

Mass Mailings: Are They Right for You?

A mass mailing—a not-so-personal job-hunting tool—is a large mailing (100 or more résumés) to potential employers. Traditionally, mass mailings have a low response rate. You may only hear from six or seven firms if you mail to 100, and you would be extremely lucky to hear from as many as ten. In today's tough market, many disappointed graduates get no responses at all from mass mailings.

Employers tend to dismiss résumés that look as if they are part of mass mailings. They have 100 résumés from new graduates on their desks to begin with, so it is easy to weed out the few who didn't care enough to write a specialized letter. Given the low response rate and the fact that mass mailings are frowned upon by the very persons you are hoping to impress, you may not think there is much point to considering one at all. Some people use them successfully, however, at the start of a job hunt to develop a few leads they might not otherwise have, while others use them at the end of a disappointing job hunt when they figure they have nothing to lose. No one can tell you whether or not a mass mailing is right for you, but if you decide to send one, there are a couple of things you can do to increase the response rate.

First, you can—and should—make even a mass mailing look personal even though this involves extra expense. You do this with a cover letter. Most copy services now have electronic typewriters that can type the same letter and put in different headings. Assuming that all your letters are going to people in the same industry, you may be able to write a cover letter that cleverly disguises the fact that it is part of a mass mailing.

The second way to set up a mass mailing—one expensive in time rather than money—is to actually write individual cover letters. If you decide to do this, you might send smaller mass mailings, perhaps only twenty-five to fifty at a shot. This is a major undertaking, much more effort than simply sending out your quota of five or six letters a week, but if you are looking for a job in an area where jobs are scarce, you may eventually end up contacting 100 or more companies anyway, and you might do better to organize yourself and do it all at once in a personalized mass mailing.

If you are willing to work very hard, you may be able to write four or five cover letters that apply to all the categories of companies you want to contact. You could then code the letters to the companies and even expand this kind of mailing to several hundred companies. You can still use an electronic typewriter to cut the time involved in preparing the letters, but if you do use one (or a personal computer or word processor) to prepare cover letters of any kind, be sure the printer is letter-quality. Using a dot-matrix printer has become a tip-off to prospective employers that this letter or résumé was mass-produced.

To Whom Do You Send Cover Letters?

Ideally, cover letters should be sent to the person who has the power to hire you. You may think this means the person at the very top, who does indeed have the power to hire you, but this isn't the case. Send a cover letter to the person who would be your immediate boss. Sometimes, this is the name given in an advertisement, or the name of someone to contact given you with a job lead.

If you are making cold calls, ask the receptionist for the department you think you want to work in. When you get someone in that department on the phone, briefly identify yourself and state that you are looking for a job in such-and-such an area. That person will often transfer you to the person who will hire you if there are any jobs, or he or she may tell you that nothing is available. Sometimes even though no job is available at the moment, you can turn the call into a fishing expedition by asking whom you would speak to if you were to call back in a month.

Whenever you prepare a cover letter, be sure to obtain the correct name and title of the person to whom you are writing. Never send a cover letter that is addressed to a title only ("To the President") or that starts "To Whom It May Concern."

If you don't have a name, a good way to find one is in one of the directories mentioned in Chapter 2. But don't stop with lifting a name out of a directory: People change jobs rather frequently today, and it's just as embarrassing to have an outdated name as to have no name at all. Call the company and ask if the person still works there. A receptionist or secretary will generally give you this information, no questions asked. If someone does ask why you are requesting the information, simply say you are planning to send the person a letter. Even if you need to spend extra time, it is worth the effort to make sure you have gotten the name of someone who actually works at the company, preferably someone with the power to hire you.

Hard Sell in a Cover Letter: Pushing Y-O-U

The cover letter is also where you should play up any of your special skills or achievements. When doing this, however, remember whom the cover letter is intended for—a prospective employer. Don't describe the job you want; describe the worker he wants and needs. A frequently heard complaint, voiced by personnel managers and executives who interview new graduates, is this one, which came from the director of personnel for a Fortune 500 company: "Young people come in here all the time prepared to tell me what they want in a job. Only rarely does someone come in whose primary interest lies in finding out what the company is looking for, and who then tries to tell me how he might fit in. But this is always the person I send upstairs for an interview with a department head."

If you have trouble pointing out a special skill or talent, which is certainly not unusual in a new graduate, then there is another approach. If you have done your homework and know what the company where you're applying is up to, then you might point out some achievement or quality of the company that makes it appealing to you. Sally, who had just gotten her master's degree in personnel, with a specialty in company benefits, knew that a particular company was high on her list of prospective employers because they had been so innovative in expanding their recreational benefits program. She told them so in a cover letter that got her a much-sought-after interview and eventually a job:

> Your company was mentioned repeatedly in a graduate seminar I took on employee benefits, and I also spent a few hours in the library reading even more about your unusual program of offering a lunchtime educational program. I am especially interested in this new trend in benefits and would, of course, like to work for the company that pioneered in this area.

Her kudos are low key but flattering. She states directly that she would like to work there, but doesn't make the assumption that there will be a job for her. Although she does not offer them a special skill or talent, she has revealed her intellectual curiosity and ambition more subtly by letting the company know that she made an extra, unassigned trip to the library to learn more about them. It is not as impressive as announcing that you did a paper on the subject of educational benefits (something Sally would definitely have included, had she done this), but a point is made nonetheless.

For this method to work, you must have done your homework and become aware of some very specific activity or product that the company is involved with. This approach will not work as well if you rather generally mention that you know the company is a leader in its field or that you know they have a reputation for being the best in their field. Try to use key words such as "led," "pioneered," "developed," or "were the first." Just be sure that what follows is some specific activity and not something so general that it could be said about any ten companies.

The Format of a Cover Letter

Although a cover letter should be personalized in the ways just discussed, it is not a "personal" letter. It is a business letter, and that means it should follow a business-letter format. Here is a sample cover letter:

> 587 Tremont Street
> Indianapolis, Indiana 49744
> September 12, 19__

Mr. William Jamison
Mutual Life Insurance Company
690 Meridian Lane
Indianapolis, Indiana 49744

Dear Mr. Jamison:

Thank you very much for meeting with me last Thursday. I was very impressed with your training program, as I had been told I would be by Bob Jones. I hope you will keep me in mind for any future openings.

> Sincerely,
>
> *Kevin Greene*
> Kevin Greene

The heading and inside address should be as complete as possible. Use abbreviations only for titles such as *Mr., Mrs.,* or *Ms.* and for *Inc.* and *Ltd. Company* should be spelled out. Spell out street names and the words *street, avenue,* and *boulevard.* If a title or address is too long for one line, continue it on the next line, indenting two or three spaces.

The greeting used to be a relatively simple business, but today you have to decide whether to use *Miss, Mrs.,* or *Ms.* A good rule of thumb is this: If a woman works, and she has enough power to hire you, she probably finds *Ms.* a perfectly acceptable and even preferable greeting. Furthermore, so many women retain the use of their maiden names that you are in a sense playing it safe to use *Ms.* It is not a good idea to use first names when writing persons whom you don't know. Only if the person is known to you and usually addressed by his or her first name—in other words, only if it would look strange to revert to Mr. or Ms. Brown—should you use the first name in a business letter.

The body of a cover letter should never run more than one page. There is no urgent need to order second sheets with your business stationery.

Possible closings are "Sincerely," "Sincerely yours," "Cordially," and "Respectfully." The best and most noncommittal is "Sincerely."

In the signature, unless the person to whom you are writing knows you personally, sign your full name. The name you sign should always match the name typed below it. And in a business letter your name should always be typed three or so lines below the closing. You have the option of using your full name, along with any "juniors" or numerical designations, or just your name alone. What you should not use are nicknames, nor should you add any formal taglines such as "Esq." or "Ph.D." The only exception is a physician, who does use "M.D." with his or her name on business stationery. Law degrees do not go after your name; they appear on your résumé. If you opt for your full, formal name—William Williamson IV—on the imprint at the top of the page, you can sign William Williamson as your signature. That may in fact be the slightly friendlier and less imposing way of introducing yourself. Don't sign "Bill Williamson" on a letter to someone whom you have never met.

These may seem to be picky little formalities, but they are also a sign that you know the ropes of business correspondence, and every little bit helps when you don't have fifteen years of experience and job skills.

What to Say in a Cover Letter

Now that you have learned about the form of a cover letter, it is time to turn your attention to what to say, something not nearly as intimidating as it may seem, especially if you use the following four-step approach. Every cover letter should contain the following:

1. A statement that you would like to work for the company, in which the company is mentioned by name
2. The reason that you would like to work for the company
3. A statement describing what you can offer the company
4. A request for an interview

Here is a sample cover letter in which all four of these steps are incorporated:

448 Riverside Drive
West Hartford, CT 06119
March 3, 19—

Mr. William Sarton
Senior Partner, Tax Division
Sarton, Sarton & Sarton,
   Counselors at Law
1300 Main Street
Princeton, New Jersey 18540

Dear Mr. Sarton:

I am writing to inquire whether there are any openings with Sarton, Sarton & Sarton.

I have long admired your work in tax law, and have always hoped that one day it might be possible for me to obtain a position with the firm.

I recently completed my master's degree in law at Yale. I took three courses on tax law and attended a seminar, in which you participated, on tax law for midsized corporations. During the summer of 1983, I was fortunate enough to obtain an internship in the New York IRS office, Corporate Division.

I shall be in the New York-New Jersey area to interview during the week of April 20–27, and I hope it will be possible for us to meet during that time to discuss any openings at Sarton, Sarton &

Sarton. I can be reached by letter at the above address or by telephone at (212) 123-4567, and I shall also take the liberty of calling your office in about ten days to see whether it will be possible for us to meet.

Sincerely,

Maria Sayers

Maria Sayers

This is an unusual cover letter in that it is more specific than most, but its author has already determined that she would like to work in tax law, and that this is perhaps the finest firm in which to learn this particular area of law. In a sense, she is gambling by being so specific about her area of interest, for she may not even be considered for other jobs in the firm, but there is a greater chance that her gamble will pay off with the job she wants.

It is to your advantage to say you will call a few days after your letter has been received to see if you can set up an interview. This leaves you with some control over the situation.

The interview is scheduled at the company's option and convenience. When, however, you are going to be in a city for only a few days specifically to interview for jobs, it is acceptable to mention the dates when you will be there in a cover letter. Most companies, especially if they are interested in talking with you, will arrange to see you during that period, if possible. If you already live in the city where you are interviewing, you have to take an interview whenever the company wants to schedule it.

Sample Cover Letters

Since cover letters can be difficult to write, here are two samples to help you get started. In the sample that follows a new graduate who really has very little to offer in the way of actual job experience has written a cover letter that still manages to play up his strengths.

5970 King Drive South
Chicago, Illinois 60628
September 1, 19—

Mr. Sidney Graham
Director of Personnel
CRT Manufacturing, Inc.
1900 Corporate Lane
Baltimore, Maryland 21200

Dear Mr. Graham:

I am writing to inquire about the possibility of obtaining a job in CRT's personnel management training program.

My special interest in your program derives from the fact that I have spent a major part of this year working on a master's thesis about new personnel techniques developed at CRT.

I am currently completing my M.B.A. at the University of Chicago, with a specialty in personnel.

I shall be in Baltimore on September 20 and 21, and wonder if we might meet to discuss this further at that time. I shall call your office next week to see about the possibility of confirming an appointment.

Sincerely,
Jack Danielson, Jr.
Jack Danielson, Jr.

The cover letter that follows is a response to a blind ad. Such ads are always difficult to respond to because you know virtually nothing about the company you are writing to. In situations like this, the following is about the best you can do, unless the ad gives a specific clue that, in turn, permits you to play up a specific skill or talent you have.

20 East Ninety-fourth Street
New York, New York 10022
December 7, 19___

Box 201
St. Louis *Courier-Journal*
St. Louis, Missouri 38470

Dear Sir or Madam:

This letter is in response to your ad of Sunday, December 3, 19___, in the *Louisville Courier-Journal*. I feel that I may have many of the qualifications you are seeking, and am enclosing a copy of my résumé, which describes my work experience and training in detail.

I would welcome the opportunity to meet with you personally to discuss your requirements for filling this position.

Sincerely,

Tania Oblesky

Although cover letters are very important and often difficult to write, with practice you will become quite adept at writing them. There is a pattern to most cover letters that makes them similar to one another. And in time, you may even come to consider it a challenge to write a cover letter that cannot be ignored.

5

The Right Kind of Résumé

A résumé is a selling tool—and it sells you. Its entire purpose is to point out and describe the special skills and talents you have that make you a viable job candidate. A résumé is intended to help you persuade a potential employer that you are someone special—someone he or she should want to hire. To write a good selling piece like this, you should allow three to four days of fairly steady work.

Trends in Résumé Writing

Only a few years ago, a résumé was fertile ground for any applicant's overactive imagination. No college degree? Well, maybe

57

you could add just one little one on your résumé, a junior college perhaps, tucked in right after high school where it would be noticed, but not . . . obvious. Were you a member of the typing pool trying to make the leap into the ranks of administrative assistants? Well, maybe you could expand just a bit on your responsibilities. After all, as long as you still had the job, no potential employer was going to call your present employer, so a little puffery was perfectly safe. And what about references? Employers *never* bothered to check them, so why not claim that you resigned from your last job when you were, in fact, fired?

Antics like these were relatively easy to get away with until a couple of years ago when employers decided they had had it with outrageously puffed résumés and began to clamp down. Too many people were not turning out to be what their résumés claimed they were.

Today, an employer is very likely to find out exactly where you went to school and even how well you did there, as well as what you did on any and all jobs you have ever held. Employers often check references very carefully these days. Today, many employers hire "conditionally," the condition being that all the data on your résumé must check out, or you are out of a job. As a new graduate, your hiring may also be conditional, depending on how your transcript looks when it arrives.

Somewhat ironically, there will never be another time in your career when you will be more tempted to puff up a résumé than when you have just graduated. If you are like 99 percent of all new graduates, you simply don't have much to put on a résumé. You will have to work to stretch it to one full page. It is important to resist this urge, and it is foolish to put in anything not honest and accurate. Keep in mind that most new graduates have very little to put on a résumé, so you are all in the same boat—the competition can't beat you on this one.

Résumés in general have very little personality these days. A lot more attention is, therefore, focused on other aspects of a résumé: grammar, spelling, strong but plain writing, format. All these topics will be covered later in this chapter, but first, let's take a look at at what makes a new graduate's résumé special, as well as some of the problems that must be solved when writing your first résumé.

What's Special About a New Graduate's Résumé?

When you have been working for a few years, your résumé will look different from the one you write as a new graduate. Then you will have some hard-core work experience and some special skills to sell to a potential employer, and this is what you will play up on a résumé. Right now, however, these are the very things you lack. But this doesn't mean you are unemployable or that your résumé cannot work for you as a selling tool—it simply must sell you in a slightly different way.

The first thing your résumé should do is to sell your potential as an employee. It should convey the idea that you are an active, intelligent, curious, ambitious person who will tackle any job with diligence. Some of the items that help to paint this picture are your class ranking, your extracurricular activities, your interests, and, of course, your descriptions of any past work experience.

Don't worry that you have only worked as a clerk in a hardware store or that you were a summer aide in a hospital back when you thought you wanted to be a doctor, even though you now have an English degree. Your past jobs show important things about you, not least of which is that you have some experience with the real world of work. The fact that you clerked in a hardware store while getting a degree in mechanical engineering shows that you were able to hold down a job and attend school at the same time and that you had the ambition to help pay your way through school. The fact that you took a summer job in a hospital even though you decided not to be a doctor shows that you were at least interested in doing something to explore your future options. Think about your summer jobs as you list them, consider what they did for you, and briefly describe their benefits or what you learned from them.

Apart from showing off potential skills as an employee, a new graduate's résumé should help him or her to form a bond with potential employers. To this end, your résumé will contain several sections—most notably on your outside interests and extracurricular activities—that would never appear on the résumé of someone who works full-time. In fact, these categories will only appear on your résumé this time; the next time you look for a job they should be dropped. But for now, when a potential employer cannot talk skills or experience with you, he or she may be attracted to you because of some common or shared experience, such as the fact that you both belonged to the same fraternity, both played in the university band, or both played intercollegiate soccer.

Finally, you need to consider what potential employers like to see—or, as the case may be, what they do not like to see—on the résumés of new graduates. In a recent survey of personnel managers by the Employment Management Association, the following advice was offered to new graduates with regard to their résumés:

- Keep it short. About 87 percent of those polled thought the ideal length for a new graduate's résumé was one page, two pages *only* if the person had extensive work experience.
- Don't name references. New graduates, more than any other category of job seeker, seem to want to list their references on the résumé, maybe because they were so important in helping students get into school or into the right clubs. It does not work that way in the world of work, although not for any special reason. It is just a custom that you not list references on your résumé, one that shows you are savvy to the world of work. Only 4 percent of those polled wanted to see references on a résumé.
- Never mention salary. This is another trap too many new graduates fall into. Even though the trend today is for employers to ask people to name a salary range or even a specific figure when they apply for a job,

personnel managers advise that new graduates especially avoid this.

- Think twice before including a job objective, which is a short description of the kind of job you are seeking. Excellent on the résumés of more experienced workers, it is often too constricting for you. Personnel experts thought new graduates should, for the most part, omit them on their résumés.

What Kind of Résumé Should You Write?

There are several styles of résumés, but one is particularly well suited to a new graduate. The basic kinds of résumé are (1) chronological, (2) skills- or achievement-oriented, and (3) creative.

The Creative Résumé

Let us begin by discussing the one that is most easily dismissed— the creative résumé—which revolves around a gimmick. A woman who wanted a job as an assistant food editor with a major newspaper sent box lunches to the food editor and the managing editor with her résumé typed out on the napkin. A man who wanted a job with an advertising agency as an illustrator described himself in a set of cartoon drawings—that was his résumé. A woman who wanted a job with a magazine wrote a query letter, a proposal that is used to sell magazine articles, in which she described herself as she would if she were proposing to write her life story.

As you can see, the gimmicks *are* sometimes clever, and they *do* sometimes get applicants jobs—especially jobs in advertising or some other traditionally "creative" area. But a creative résumé bombs more often than it succeeds, and it usually is not worth ruining your chances with 100 potential employers to find the one zany enough to appreciate your own brand of zaniness. Besides, even if you find the one employer in 100 to hire you on the basis of your having presented him with an outrageous résumé, then what have you really accomplished? More often than not, you've gotten

yourself a flaky employer—and that may only spell trouble several
months down the road. Skip the creative résumé. If you are the
hotshot who's going to set the advertising world on its head in the
eighties, that's great, but there are other ways to get started than
by cooking up a gimmicky résumé.

The Skills- or Achievement-Oriented Résumé

The other kind of résumé you won't want to use, although for entirely different reasons, is the skills- or achievement-oriented
résumé. This type of résumé is organized entirely around work
achievements or special skills that a job seeker has to offer, and
because of this, is too sophisticated for most new graduates. Unless
you are a highly unusual graduate, you probably do not have the
special skills or the work background to show off in this type of
résumé.

The Chronological Résumé

The kind of résumé that *is* ideally suited to the new graduate is the
chronological résumé, in which you describe yourself, your education, and your work experience in straightforward, chronological
order. Here is an example:

RESUME

PERSONAL   Marvin Brye
1345 Brilton Lane
Norwich, Connecticut 06360
Phone: (203) 888-8367

Will relocate

EDUCATION   M.S., Foods and Nutrition, 1984
Cum laude
Connecticut State College

B.S., Institutional Management, 1982
Connecticut State College

WORK EXPERIENCE   Internship, Connecticut State Hospital and
Nursing Home Facility, 1983
Internship was divided into rotating services.
I elected to work in gerontology, patient
diet education, meal service, and outpatient
counseling.

For four summers, I also worked at the
Connecticut State Nursing Home Facility as
a junior chef and during the last year as
a diet counselor.

MILITARY SERVICE   U.S. Marine Corps, 1974–78, honorably
discharged with rank of corporal. I
worked as a paramedic and I was stationed in
Alabama, California, and West Germany.

LICENSE   Licensed in Connecticut, New Jersey, and
New York

REFERENCES   References available on request

If this kind of résumé still looks too plain for your tastes, here is
another kind you can write—an expanded chronological résumé.

MARGIE RUBENSTEIN

School address:
123 Evans Avenue
Iowa City, Iowa 52242
(319) 348-6666

Address after May 16, 1984:
1001 Eighteenth Avenue
Omaha, Nebraska 68102
(515) 858-3174

JOB OBJECTIVE

Advertising-assistant position with possible advancement to a career as an account executive.

EDUCATION

B.A., May 1984, University of Iowa. Concentrations in Journalism and Marketing. Earned 50 percent of college expenses; carried full academic load every semester.

Course Highlights: Marketing Communications, Consumer Behavior, Theory/Practice of Persuasion, Advertising Theory/Planning, News Editing, Graphic Arts, Organizing Mass Communication Productions.

EXPERIENCE

Advertising and Reporting: Advertising Intern (summer 1983), Sun Newspapers of Omaha. Responsibilities were handling and servicing various account departments, advertising director's accounts, designing and laying out ads, selling ad space, and working in traffic control. Feature Reporter (summer 1982), *Eldora Herald Index*. Wrote feature articles, covered city council meetings, set headlines, sold and laid out advertising for a special insert. Stencil Designer (summer 1981), Dodger Gym Manufacturing. Designed in-house stencils for customer orders and stenciled athletic wear. Standing job with Dodger Gym for all semester and spring breaks.

Other Work Experience: Hostess/Waitress, Shipping Department Clerk, Crew Boss.

PUBLICATIONS/PROJECTS

Feature stories, *Eldora Herald Index;* two articles, School of Journalism *Lab Tabs;* editor of four-page tabloid; editor of marketing-research analysis project for Hardee's; advertisements, *Eldora Herald Index* and Sun newspapers; now in progress, twenty-minute documentary film.

HONORS/AWARDS

University of Iowa athletic scholarship, scholarship loan from Miriam Brown Educational Trust Fund, Dolphin Queen candidate.

COLLEGE ACTIVITIES

Member/team captain Women's Intercollegiate Basketball Team, intramural athletics; elected member, Greek Expansion Task Force; publications/historian, Pi Beta Phi; director, Campus March of Dimes Fund Drive.

STRENGTHS

Energetic, work well under pressure, very willing to accept responsibility, have great perseverance.

REFERENCES/PORTFOLIO

References available at Career Services and Placement Center, Iowa Memorial Union, University of Iowa, Iowa City, Iowa 52242, (319) 353-3147. Portfolio available upon request.

As you work on your résumé, don't let yourself become discouraged because you don't have years of experience or a specialized skill that will help you land a job. The fact that you are weak in these two areas simply means that you must sell yourself in other areas, namely, on your willingness to learn and your belief that you will be a valuable employee to whoever hires you.

What Goes in a Résumé

All résumés contain certain elements of information, which are listed below. After you have finished your résumé, use this as a checklist to make sure you haven't omitted anything.

- ☐ Name, address, and telephone number
- ☐ Job objective (optional)
- ☐ Work experience
- ☐ Language skills
- ☐ Education
- ☐ Publications
- ☐ Extracurricular activities and personal interests (optional and only included on your first résumé)
- ☐ Record of military service
- ☐ Professional memberships
- ☐ Note about willingness to travel
- ☐ Note about willingness to relocate
- ☐ Statement about references

Especially since this is your first résumé, you may find it helpful to read a little more about each of these items so you can understand how they work in a résumé.

Name, address, and telephone number. Although this may seem too obvious to mention, you would not believe the number of résumés that are immediately condemned to the wastebasket simply because there is no address or telephone number. The person who receives them obviously has no idea how to contact the job seeker. Double-check to be sure you don't make this wasteful mistake.

Job objective. As discussed earlier, a job objective is often too limiting on a new graduate's résumé. You almost certainly will not want to include one if you are a liberal arts major, but if you have studied in a highly specialized area of science or engineering, for example, you may decide to state a job objective. Whatever you do, if you do list a job objective, don't describe a job that you can't possibly get, either because you lack the qualifications for it or are too inexperienced. Sometimes new graduates have an overinflated idea of the kind of work they can actually do, and this often comes out in the job objective. Don't use a job objective to put forth unrealistic expectations ("I hope to obtain a mid-level management position that puts me in a direct line to a vice presidency"). A job objective should only be used to narrow the field of employment or to pinpoint a specialization ("I am seeking an entry-level job in a small- to medium-sized company specializing in metallurgical engineering").

Work experience. If you have some substantial work experience under your belt, this should be the next section on your résumé. If not, then work experience should follow the education section. If you don't have any work experience, don't manufacture anything; just omit this section. On the other hand, don't forget that internships, summer jobs, and volunteer work are all valid work experience.

Language skills. Be sure to describe any language skills you have, as well as your level of fluency, but don't exaggerate. If you are hired because you claim you're fluent in Spanish when you really need an hour to decipher one short letter, you will probably find yourself on the street job hunting again. On the other hand, if you have any language skills, even if you do not plan to make a career of them, don't underestimate their possible value in helping you to get that first job.

Education. If this is the most important thing you have to offer an employer, then it should be the very first item on your résumé after your name, address, and telephone number. The education section is straightforward. Include your high school education only if you want to use it to show off your academic abilities. Then you should include the name of the high school, the city and state, the year you graduated, and your class ranking or the fact that you made the honor roll or whatever the equivalent was in your school. Don't include high school activities on a résumé once you have a college education. The format for your higher education should match that of high school: name of institution, city and state, and year of graduation. If you have not yet graduated, write:

Iowa State University, Ames, Iowa
Will graduate with B.S., January 1984

Be sure to include your degree or degrees, and on your first résumé (and maybe any others you write over the next few years), add your major and minor. List your class rank or "cum laude" or "magna cum laude" last. Omit your class rank if it isn't high. What is considered a high class rank varies from year to year (depending on the job market), the school you attended, and your course of study. Ask around among fellow students whose course of study is similar to yours, and find out where the cutoff point seems to be. Check with a career placement officer to see what he or she advises.

Extracurricular activities and personal interests. As a general rule, these are the first items to be dropped from a résumé when you gain some work experience. For the time being, however, they can be valuable selling tools. Don't go into any great detail; just list your activities and interests in a straightforward manner, as is done on the sample résumés. Also list any elected offices or particular achievements you accomplished in connection with your extracurricular activities.

Record of military service. If you have any military service under your belt, be sure to note that on your résumé, including the ROTC. If you were honorably discharged or received any special training, add that, too. If for any reason you received a less than honorable discharge, you should still mention your military service, but not the discharge. Legally, an employer cannot ask you about it.

Professional memberships. These are not the same thing as extracurricular activities, although they sometimes overlap. If you have a junior or associate membership in any professional organization, then either list it under a separate section or if it will give your résumé a cleaner look, list it with your extracurricular activities. Sometimes, for example, adding one section that contains only one line of information only clutters up the résumé, so in situations like this, where the items are similar, combine the two sections.

Willingness to travel. If you are willing to travel on the job, note this on the résumé (see samples).

Willingness to relocate. Since most college graduates are willing—and even eager—to leave their college towns or hometowns, you will probably want to add a sentence about this. Actually, you are not "relocating" as much as you are "locating." Be careful about limiting yourself to one part of the country. If you prefer to live—and hope you will end up living—on the East Coast, then maybe add a sentence to the effect on the résumés that you plan to send to the East Coast. It may make those companies look at you a little more seriously. But you should also prepare a résumé that is more general. You don't want to be disqualified for a great job in San Francisco, do you, because of a geographic limitation? Even if you are fairly inflexible about where you will live, it is probably better not to announce this on a résumé.

Don't add any flip statements or outrageous aspirations about your willingness to live anywhere on the Planet Earth. International assignments are plums, and they rarely go to new graduates. If you are doing your best to get an international assignment, that is still not something you announce on your résumé. The best solution, whatever you want, is to add the simple sentence "Willing to relocate" to your résumé, if you must say anything.

References. As noted, you never give references on a résumé, but rather, you add a line that reads: "References available on request."

How Many Résumés Do You Need?

Before you start writing a résumé, take a minute to consider how many you will need—not how many copies you will have printed (that is covered later in the chapter), but how many different résumés will be necessary in your job search. Are you an English major who wants to work in business so you can decide whether or not you want to go on for an M.B.A.? But then, would you also take—in fact, would you love to find—a job in publishing? Then you will need at least two résumés—one geared toward a job in publishing, the other toward one in business. Or perhaps you are a biologist with two areas of specialization who may want two résumés, each emphasizing a different area. Are you determined eventually to live in the Denver area, but you wouldn't turn down a chance to spend a few years in the Big Apple? You should write one résumé in which you say you hope to locate in or near Denver and another one for East Coast job leads.

Most people can get by with one general, all-purpose résumé which they adapt as individual opportunities arise. Suppose, for example, that you hear about a great job with a small solar energy company. You should definitely take the time to write a résumé slanted toward that particular job and include any especially relevant facts. Did you write a paper on conserving energy in your dorm, or do some volunteer work for a short while (too short a while to mention on your general résumé, you decided) with a conservation group? By all means, write a special résumé that plugs these specific experiences into the company's needs.

The one time you may want to include a job objective is when you write a special résumé to help you get one particular job. In the job just mentioned, it is somewhat manipulative but definitely worth the effort, for example, to add a job objective noting that you hope to find work "in a small to medium-sized company in the field of energy or conservation." Keep the job objective a little more general than the specific job, however, or it will look contrived.

How to Start Writing Your Résumé

Begin by roughing out what you want to say, based on the checklist of items to include. Next, type a rough copy, trying to arrange the material as you type so that it is pleasing to the eye.

Note that a résumé consists of blocks of descriptive copy as well as headlines. These sections should all be as parallel to each other as possible. For example, if you capitalize "Education," then you should also capitalize "Work Experience," and "Extracurricular Activities."

Résumés are often written in a kind of shorthand language in which no "person" is used. You don't use "I," in other words. (See the sample of the expanded chronological résumé.) Regardless of whether or not you use the first person, use the same form consistently in all the copy blocks. Don't jump back and forth between two styles as this writer does:

> Summer, 1981. Clerked at Simpson's Department store, toy department.
>
> Summer, 1982. I enjoyed the opportunity to work in a local volunteer project for hunger.

A better way to write this material would be:

> Summer, 1981. Clerk, Simpson's Department Store. I worked in toys, where my responsibilities included waiting on customers, operating the cash register, and occasionally working in the stock room.
>
> Summer, 1982. Volunteer, Hunger, Inc. I worked on a unique project to distribute food to needy women with small chil-

dren, and my responsibilities included helping mothers fill out
the application forms required to obtain the service, deliv-
ering food, and discussing nutrition.

Note, too, that if you describe one job, you must describe all your
jobs to approximately the same degree. You should not simply list
one job and then write a glowing description of another one.

Basically, résumé language should be plain. Always go for the
simple word or expression over the fancier one. Don't say you "in-
terfaced" with customers when you mean you "worked" with
them. Do try to use action verbs as much as possible. For example,
say "I designed" (or "planned," "initiated," or "improved") rather
than the more static "I was" or "I worked at."

Your résumé must also be written with impeccable grammar—
and that includes perfect spelling. There is no way around it. One
misspelled word, one sloppy grammatical construction, and your
résumé will most likely land in the wastebasket before it has even
been read through once. This is a tough order, but it is the way the
world of work operates. If you cannot take the time to write a
grammatically perfect and perfectly spelled résumé, then, unfortunately, no employer will think you are the proper candidate for
more serious work. It's like showing up in an unpressed suit for a
job interview. Ask a friend or someone who you know is good at
grammar and spelling to take a careful look at your last draft before the final typing is done.

The final important thing to keep in mind as you write your
résumé is to phrase everything in as positive a way as you possibly
can. This may sound easy, but in fact many writers have a ten-
dency to put things in a negative rather than a positive light. For
example:

> Although I wasn't magna cum laude, I graduated 50th in a
> class of 250.

Instead, write:

> Graduated 50th in a class of 250.

Don't write:

> Not available for full-time work until June 1984.

Instead, write:

> Available for work in June 1984.

Always check your résumé to be sure you have stated everything in as positive a way as you possibly can.

Writing Rough Drafts—Lots of Them

Don't panic if you feel inept as you begin to write your résumé, or if you find yourself unsuccessfully juggling both what to say and how to arrange it on the page. Keep at it, and don't give up. This is the tinkering stage, and if you tinker long enough, a shape will emerge.

The key to producing a thoughtful, concise résumé is to write lots of rough drafts. If possible, type out the later drafts so you can arrange the résumé as it will actually look on the typewritten page when it is finished. Keep working until you get it exactly right.

When you think you have finished your résumé, put it away for a few days. When you get it out, you will look at with a fresh eye and may spot some areas that need fixing. Also, never send out a résumé that someone else has not reviewed for you—not because you are a new graduate or inexperienced; this is sound advice for anyone writing a résumé.

A Professional Touch for Your Résumé

If you cannot type well, hire someone to type the final copy for you. Resist the urge, however, to use anything more elaborate than typewriter type. Résumés that look too professional—as if they have been typeset, for example—are frowned upon in almost every field. If your résumé is too fancy, employers will think you had a service do it for you, and that is unacceptable. Employers want to see an example of your work in your résumé.

Once you have a final typed draft, you are ready to have your résumé reproduced, which is perfectly acceptable as long as you obtain high-quality copies. (You can also send out individually typed résumés, if you prefer to.) There are two ways to reproduce your résumé: copying and printing. Go to any copy center and check out the prices for both copying and what is called "instant printing." If you are planning to make fifty or fewer copies, copying is probably the cheapest method. If you are planning a mass mailing or need more than fifty copies, depending on the individual copy center's prices, it may be cheaper to use instant printing, which produces a printed copy from your typed copy. It is done in bulk, and usually costs $7 to $8 per 100 copies. Copying, by contrast, costs about 7 to 10 cents a page.

Resist the urge to print your résumé on colored stock. Buy a good bond paper (usually you can get this from whoever does the copying or instant printing), preferably one that is similar in quality to your stationery.

Also resist the urge to include a photo of yourself. It is simply not professional. Many people want to do it because they are especially good-looking and think this will help them get a job, or because they think attaching a photo will help to set them apart from the rest of the crowd. However, this is a clear sign that you do not yet know your way around the real world of work, and such a tactic is more likely to backfire.

When you have your copies in hand, you are ready to start mailing them out to prospective employers. As you do this, remember:

- Always enclose a cover letter.
- Always put the proper amount of postage on it.
- Fold the résumé neatly in thirds and mail it in a No.

10 envelope that matches your cover letter, or leave it flat and mail it in a large envelope. (One school of thought maintains that a résumé and cover letter in a large envelope are more noticeable and thus are slated for immediate attention, but there is no definite proof of this.)

Instant Death to Your Résumé

Finally, there are a few things that will propel your résumé directly into the wastebasket.

- Poor grammar
- Misspelling of any kind
- Handwritten letter or résumé
- Failure to include your name, address, and telephone number
- Poor copies of your résumé (so it looks as if it is the one-thousandth copy)
- Unrealistic job goals
- Unrealistic salary or job expectations
- Vagueness, especially in describing your education or work experience
- Too much puffery, especially describing responsibilities clearly beyond your age or past experience
- Anything written on onionskin paper
- Too long (usually, that means anything over one page)

6

When and How to Let Ma Bell Help Out

There is a time to use the telephone during a job search—and a time not to use it. Unfortunately, the very times when you shouldn't use it are usually the ones when you sit anxiously by the phone waiting for that all-important call that will result in the job of your dreams. The telephone may help you in your job search when you make the initial contact, the follow-up call after you have mailed a cover letter and résumé, and a well-timed call or two after a job interview.

Should You Use the Phone for an Initial Contact?

Experts disagree about the initial use of the phone even for experienced job hunters. Some say a letter and résumé only get lost, so if you really want to stand out, you should pick up the phone and introduce yourself. Others say the person you call will only talk to you because he or she feels guilty or obligated, not good circumstances for an introduction. In general, it is probably best for new graduates *not* to use a telephone for initial contacts if they can help it. For one thing, you are probably too young to have enough authority to get through to the person with the power to hire you. And for another thing, you don't have enough job experience so that most employers will be jumping to see you; it's too easy to say no to someone who calls out of the blue. Far better to go through "regular" channels, i.e., a cover letter and a résumé followed by a phone call, than to try to brazen your way from the beginning with a call.

There is, however, one time when you must use the telephone for an initial contact, and that is when you hear about a great job a little bit too late. Perhaps the company is about to stop interviewing, or maybe they have been interviewing for several weeks and are about to wrap up the search and choose someone. And you have only just heard about the job! If the job is of great interest to you, and if you have reason to believe that the company will be interested in you, then by all means telephone. When you do this, explain—briefly—why you are calling so late. You may have to offer an explanation to the secretary in order to get through to the boss, and you certainly should offer a brief explanation to the top brass when he or she answers your call. Say something like this:

> "Ms. Smithson, I'm sorry to call so late about his job. I understand that you have been interviewing for several weeks now, but I only heard about the job yesterday from a friend, and I would very much like to meet with you, if possible. I'm fluent in French and have a good working knowledge of Spanish, and I'm eager to work as a translator. I also know of ABC

Translators, Inc., and your excellent reputation, and I'll be very disappointed to miss out on one of your rare entry-level jobs."

If a statement like this one doesn't melt the heart of the toughest employer, then he or she probably isn't worth working for.

Do keep your explanation brief, and don't sound as if you are begging for an interview. Also make sure your explanation is honest, with one exception: Don't say anything that puts you in a bad light. If you missed the ABC Translators, Inc., newspaper ad because you took a week off to work on your tan and did not buy the newspaper—while your friend Judy, who was interviewing in another city 400 miles away, still managed to buy the local newspaper every day so she wouldn't miss any good leads and only told you about the job when she got back—*don't admit it.* Make up a white lie if possible, or don't say anything about why you didn't know about the job—and make sure you don't get caught goofing off again! Job hunting is a full-time job, and you can undoubtedly see from this situation how doing it less than full-time can hurt you.

Using a Follow-Up Phone Call

If new graduates generally should not make the initial contact by telephone, it is nonetheless a serious mistake not to follow up a cover letter and résumé with a phone call. The last thing you should expect is that potential employers will get in touch with you after receiving your cover letter and résumé. It's true that some may, but most potential employers will wait to see if you are aggressive and interested enough to follow up on your first contact.

Wait about ten days before you make the call. When you do call, ask to speak to the person to whom you sent your cover letter and résumé. And be sure to ask for the person by name. When the person comes on the line, identify yourself immediately and remind him that you are calling as you said you would in your cover letter. Then pause a few seconds and wait for the person to take control and either ask you to interview or tell you that an interview is impossible.

If the person on the other end of the wire doesn't respond right after you have identified yourself, you take control. Ask for an interview by saying something like this: "As I mentioned in my letter, my background is in electrical engineering. I developed a transistor project in college along the lines of your newest transistor radios. [In other words, plug yourself briefly.] I'd be very interested in talking with you about a job. Could we possibly meet during the next week or so to talk? [This is where you close the sale. You ask directly for what you want: an interview.] I think I might have something to offer DEF Electronics."

Getting to Yes

If you are invited for an interview, if possible, set up an appointment right then and there, although the busy executive may pass you on to a secretary or administrative assistant to arrange specifics. Be sure to repeat the time and date so you know you have them straight. Close the conversation with a pleasantry: "I am looking forward to this opportunity to meet with you." Alternately, if you are talking to a secretary, say, "I'll be there next Tuesday, October ninth, at 2:00 P.M. Thank you."

Getting to Maybe

Sometimes it's hard to know if you are getting a yes to your request for an interview. An executive may say he would like to talk to you but will be on vacation for a month or has to finish year-end financial reports. If you are not feeling aggressive, it may be easy to interpret this as a polite no. Don't let yourself do this, however. If this person doesn't want to see you, he or she owes you a more direct refusal. Otherwise, in situations like this, assume that the stalling is done in good faith and that you will get your interview eventually.

When faced with a vague "yes," try something like this:

> "I'm sorry you can't see me right away, but I understand how busy you are. When would be a good time for me to call back, or do you schedule appointments that far in advance? I'm willing to set something up right now for a month from now, if you are."

Of course, if the person does not really want to see you, you will probably get a more direct no at this point, but if he or she really wants to see you, or is, at best, ambivalent, this slight show of assertiveness on your part will usually result in an appointment for an interview.

Don't be put off if someone is ambivalent about seeing you and shows it. After all, you are just a voice on the phone, perhaps one of hundreds of new graduates who have called over the past few months. The ambivalence is normal and only to be expected. Just don't let it stop you. This is the time to push a little to get the other person to schedule an interview.

When the Answer Is No

When your request for an interview is turned down, the reason that is most often given is that there are no jobs available at the moment. Or you may be told you do not have the qualifications for a job that was advertised. If possible, try to turn the no into a yes. Ask if you can come in anyway and briefly introduce yourself in case a job opens up later. At this stage, the more you can do to become a real person to a potential employer, the more likely it is that he will remember to call you when there is a job opening. If the answer is still no, send a letter thanking the person for talking with you, and ask that your résumé be kept on file in the event that there is an opening.

Sometimes an interviewer may tell you he can't give you an interview because he doesn't have the time—another way of saying there are no jobs. Again, counter this by saying: "I understand how busy you are. Could I call you back in a few weeks when you aren't so busy and arrange to drop by just to introduce myself?" If the person says that would be all right, put a note in your files so you'll remember to call at the right time. It is a smart ploy to send this person a brief note thanking him for talking with you and reminding him that you will call again in a few weeks.

Occasionally, your request for an interview will be refused, and no reason will be given. You cannot do much with this situation. It may help to pull out a trump card and mention the special reason that the company might be interested in you—carefully couching these comments, of course, in terms of how you might be of service to the company. Or you can try to muster sympathy by commenting on how very interested you are in the company and then citing a specific reason. To do this well, you must already have done your homework and must have something concretely flattering to say about the company.

Dealing With Rejection

Often, when you are turned down for an interview, it will be done by letter. Some smart executives who want to avoid an interview get off a letter in response to a résumé stating that there are no jobs available. This may be one of those times to pick up the phone and give it one more try, anyway. Persistence frequently pays off in a job hunt. To be honest, though, getting turned down for interviews is a bit hard on the old ego, so you may want to save those phone calls for times when the company, or the job, is especially important to you. If this is one of those situations, call the person who said no, and ask if you can drop by anyway to introduce yourself in case there are future openings. Be very polite if he or she still says no, and ask to be kept in mind if any jobs at your level open up. This sometimes works.

Speaking of your ego, keep in mind that you will have to deal with a few—and perhaps many—rejections before you find the right job. Don't let yourself feel badly when the answer is no, and don't crumple into passivity when confronted with an ambivalent no that can possibly be turned into a yes. Do try to handle these situations with persistence and politeness. Whatever you do, don't let your disappointment turn into arrogance. It is better to show that you are frightened or admit your extreme disappointment over not getting an interview than to turn even the slightest bit overbearing. That's a sure way to be remembered—and never invited for a job interview.

Calls to Get Information

You will occasionally need to call a company simply to get information about a job. Your best bet is to call personnel or to ask an executive's secretary or administrative assistant. Ask a few key questions: Are there any jobs? What kind of person are they looking for? Whom should you contact to apply for the job?

Be a little discreet about announcing who you are during these foraging calls. Do give your name but don't necessarily mention that you are job hunting immediately. Wait until the person has warmed up to you a little. At that point, it is sometimes helpful to explain what you're up to; the person may take an active enough interest in you to help you get an interview.

Getting Past—and Along With—the Staff

Throughout your search for a job, you will find yourself dealing with people whom you may view as underlings. There is something very important to keep in mind when dealing with these people: No matter how fancy your college degree, you are still a notch below these people, for the very simple reason that they have a job and you don't. In fact, they have a job in a place where you would like to work. This is not meant to belittle you—just to stop you from alienating people who have more power than you think and who can make or break your budding opportunities with a company. It is a bit easy when you are feeling disappointed or not getting the overwhelmingly positive response you want to take out your disappointment on the people you consider low on the totem pole. (You also may be surprised to learn that office life isn't divided this way anymore, and that once you have a job, it still is in your best interests to be very nice to everyone with whom you have any professional contact.)

Aside from all the reasons you shouldn't alienate a secretary, there is a very good reason to have one on your side: She or he has the boss's ear. Secretaries are never quite so powerless as they are perceived to be, and in fact, one sniff to the boss from a valued secretary about your telephone manners, and you may be out of the running for a job.

When a secretary answers the phone, identify yourself before she has a chance to ask. When she does ask if she may say who is calling, respond: "I'm Jill Smith, and I'm calling to inquire about the job that was advertised in this morning's paper."

If she seems at all accessible, consider taking her into your confidence a little. For example, you might say, "Oh, Mr. Smith can't see me. I'm so disappointed. I know XYZ Co. is the leader in aeronautical engineering, and that's what my degree is in. I was really hoping just to have a chance to talk with someone there, even if there aren't any jobs right now." At that point, she or he may well put in a word with the boss about "that very nice young person who would like to talk to you," and you may get an interview. You can also ask a secretary when he thinks a job might be open. They are usually delighted to show off their knowledge, and they often know more about impending resignations than the boss does. Don't press too much, however, or take too much of a secretary's time. After all, they are busy at work, too.

The Best Time to Use the Phone

Just as there are good and bad times to schedule an interview, there are also good and bad times to make telephone calls. Calling early in the morning earns you points for being an early bird, and we all know what early birds get in this world. On the other hand, most people who work in offices appreciate having a little time to catch their breath, finish the morning paper, and settle in before the phone starts ringing. Because of this, your best bet is to call about 9:30 or 10:00 A.M. It is often easy to catch someone right before lunch, between 11:30 A.M. and noon. Most morning meetings end before lunch, and most people touch base with their desks before they go to lunch. As the day wears on people tend to become more involved in their work, and you are less likely to get through or to get someone's full attention if you do succeed in reaching him.

If a person is very hard to reach, though, try calling fifteen to thirty minutes after closing time or even before opening time. Many busy people use the hours before and after the official ones to do serious work. Admittedly, they are usually at work then because the phone will not disturb them, but if there seems to be no other way to catch someone, then try calling at those times.

Also, when you are having trouble reaching someone, solicit a secretary's help. She or he may not bother to tell you unless you ask directly, but most secretaries know exactly when to catch their bosses.

Do Gimmicks Work?

Never use any kind of gimmick when you are trying to get through to someone to talk about a job. The biggest gimmick, of course, is to say that the call is personal when it isn't. Even the toughest and most intimidating palace guard doesn't want to risk the ruler's displeasure by failing to put through his stockbroker with a hot tip or his second cousin from Omaha with a cut-rate charter airline ticket. You may get through, all right, but what you'll get through to is a very annoyed executive. And he, in turn, will take out his annoyance on his secretary, whom you so deceitfully got past, and she will thereafter view you as a dangerous enemy. For, you see, you have erred on two accounts, pulling the wool over the secretary's eyes and upsetting the boss, the very person whom she or he is to some degree expected to protect. It simply is not worthwhile ever to lie.

Practicing Your Telephone Manners— And Manner

Always keep in mind that you are only a voice on the telephone. No one can see you smiling. No one can study your body language and realize that you sound arrogant when you are merely anxious. If you have an abrupt way of speaking, it will only sound more abrupt on the phone; if you talk too fast, that fault will probably only be accelerated on the phone, as will the opposite problem, talking too slowly. (Of course, if you have a genuine speech impairment, such as a stutter, there is nothing you can do about it, and you cannot—and should not—let it keep you from using the phone in your job search.)

A little politeness goes a very long way on the phone. The magic words are "Thank you" and "Please." And think about using questions rather than statements to make requests. "Do you think I could speak with Dr. Mangold?" has a softer ring to it than a crisp "I'd like to speak to Dr. Mangold, please."

There are two ways to check out your telephone manners. Ask a friend how you sound on the phone or record yourself talking on the phone.

If you do have a problem, do something about it. Consult with a speech teacher and ask for some exercises if your voice is not as pleasant as it might be. Practice with a tape recorder to improve your speech. Practice with a friend who can advise you and help you change your speech. If you are very nervous when you talk on the phone, use a prewritten script until you have made enough calls for the apprehension to wear off. Eventually it will.

The more you talk on the phone the better you will get at it. And you will find yourself doing a lot of telephoning as you search for a job.

7

Get Ready to Interview

So far, you have done everything right, and now you are starting to get some results. In fact, your first real job interview is less than two weeks away—and you're terrified. What, if anything, should you do to get ready for this interview? And what, if anything, can you do to get rid of some of your nervousness?

There is a lot you can do to prepare for an interview, and for the moment, don't worry about the anxiety. As you will learn later, you can sometimes make it work for you during the interview.

The Key to Surviving a Job Interview

There is only one key to interviewing successfully: You must have a rap. Of course, it will matter that you have attended an Ivy

League school or graduated at the top of your class, but the single most important thing you must do in an interview is make your experience and qualifications—whatever they are—look like the right experience and qualifications for this particular job. Even if there is something that might be held against you—let's say you flunked two English courses—you should turn this into a valuable experience, one that puts forth some positive experience to counterbalance what might have been a negative one. For example, if the interviewer comments, "I'm not sure you're qualified for this job since you only have a minor in social work, and we are looking for someone who has majored in it," put your sales pitch to work by replying, "I realize I don't have exactly the experience you're seeking, but I didn't get involved in social work until my junior year, and at that point, there wasn't time left to take enough hours for a major. I did view my social work courses as my most important ones because I knew I wanted to work in this field. I also supplemented my minor by volunteering in local clinics. And I am planning to start work on a master's as soon as possible."

In short, shed some positive light on something that might be held against you and make your experience—however slight—appear to qualify you for a particular job. You can't develop your sales pitch during an interview, although there will be many occasions when you will have to think on your feet. In this chapter, as you get ready to interview, you will spend some time developing that which will work for you. To do this, you must do three things:

> Know yourself.
> Know the company.
> Know the job you want.

Knowing yourself means that you have thoroughly prepared for the interview and have a good idea how you will handle yourself. Knowing the company means that you have done a considerable amount of homework and that you can use what you have learned to show an active, thoughtful interest in the firm. Knowing the job you want is a slightly more complex undertaking for someone who has never had a job, but there are some things you can do to prepare yourself in this area, too.

Practice, Practice, Practice

The best way to predict and even control your performance during a job interview—to "know yourself," in other words—is to practice. Practice alone with a tape recorder and in front of the mirror; with friends, career counselors, and school advisers; even with throwaway interviews. Throwaway interviews are ones with companies you're pretty sure you don't want to work for. In other words, the pressure is not on you to perform well. Try to schedule three or four of these early on in your job hunt so you can see how well you perform and what you need to do to sharpen your interviewing skills.

Before you go on any interview, though, spend several days practicing. Go over the situations and questions that you are likely to encounter. (The next chapter contains a list of questions you will probably hear over and over again, as well as a list of troublesome questions you may encounter.) For example, if your grade point average isn't as good as it should have been, you know this could pose a problem during an interview. It will help to prepare an answer that emphasizes your strengths and plays down your weaknesses. Before you go into an interview you should have identified the potential problems you may encounter, and you should have rehearsed responses to troublesome questions. The questions that you will hear over and over again in every interview ("Why should I give you a job?" to name one) are easier to finesse, but they, too, still require practice.

Many people feel funny practicing in front of a mirror, and most of us feel a little awkward asking someone to check out our interviewing style. Frankly, asking for this kind of advice is a little like asking your best friend to tell you whether you have bad breath. But you will feel a lot more awkward if you are in the middle of an important job interview, and you find yourself getting increasingly nervous and out of control because you are not prepared to handle what's coming your way.

Not only should you develop some set answers to the questions you will be asked, but also you should check out your diction. Do you speak too quickly? Lapse into a monotone? These are the two main speaking problems people have when they are frightened. Does your voice have a pleasant quality, neither too loud nor too soft? If your voice is too loud, practice reducing the volume, and if you speak too softly, learn to speak up. If you have a real problem and cannot change it yourself, consult a speech teacher. You can probably get free advice from someone in your college's speech or English department, but if the problem is really serious, you may need to hire a professional consultant.

Last but hardly least, check out your body language. It tells so much about you. Most importantly, have someone evaluate your handshake and eye contact. Both may show insecurity and a lack of self-confidence, and both are relatively easy things to improve. Your handshake should be firm—period. If it is too limp, you will be viewed as a lukewarm person or someone with little personality. If it is too strong, you might be considered too aggressive or pushy.

Your body language can send other messages about you, too. While practicing everything else, you should also practice "interview posture." Start by sitting up straight in a chair—not rigidly straight but attentively straight. Don't fidget. Don't sit on your hands; if you must do something with them, slip them into your pockets. You should never put your elbows or any of your belongings on the interviewer's desk. Your briefcase and/or purse should rest in your lap or be placed on the floor leaning against your chair. Don't cross your arms; it appears hostile and closed.

Let Nervousness Work for You

The point of spending so much time on your body language and speech is to help you appear to be self-confident and at ease during the interview, but you may find, as do almost all job seekers, that you cannot entirely get rid of your nervousness during an interview. Don't worry about it. A little nervousness will work in your favor. It shows that the interview and the job are important to you, that you are really interested in working for this company and are, as a consequence, trying to do your very best in this interview.

Obviously, either too much self-confidence or too much nervousness can work against you in a job interview, but having a little of each—and letting them show—will only help you.

Do Your Homework First

As noted earlier, it is imperative that you also know the company you are interviewing with. How much you find out about a company will depend on how interested you are in a job. If you followed the suggestions in Chapter 2 and put together dossiers on the twenty or so companies you would most like to work for, you will only have to review material you already have. If you are interviewing with a company that is not in a dossier, you may have to head back to the library to see what you can learn about it.

In any interview that matters to you, you need to be as up-to-date as possible about the company. It is not really enough to know their name and their products. You should also have some idea of their sales record over the past few years, whether they are starting any new divisions or launching any new products, what their reputation is in their field, how well they treat their employees, and anything else you can find out. You should never drop names in an interview, but it won't hurt to know the names of the chairman of the board and the president as well as anyone else who has made a name for himself or herself within the company, so you can nod knowledgeably if the name is mentioned.

As you gather information, it helps to keep in mind how you will use it during an interview. Although you should become something of an expert on any company you are really interested in, you probably won't show off even 10 percent of what you have learned during an interview. But there are also subtle ways to demonstrate what you know (provided you really do know it) such as nodding when the chairman of the board's name is mentioned or responding to something the interviewer tells you by saying, "Oh, yes, I'm familiar with that," or "I read about that in an article in *Fortune.*" This is no time to bluff, though, because once you act informed about a subject, the interviewer may decide to pursue it or test your knowledge. You don't have to know everything there is to know about a company's job training program, for example, based on what you read in a *Fortune* magazine article, but you should know a fact or two that you can use once you indicate that you have done some homework. Unlike certain situations in which you can bluff, this is a time to be very sure of what you know—however limited it may be.

Know the Job You Want

This is the trickiest area for new graduates. If you're like most new graduates, you realize you will have to take any acceptable entry-level job you can get. On the other hand, you cannot admit this in an interview because it will make you look too available, too easy, and in the eyes of many interviewers, too vague about what it is you really want in a job.

You have to go into an interview with some kind of idea about what exactly you hope to obtain from the world of work. The trick is to leave the impression that you are willing and eager to work at almost any entry-level job while still having some concrete idea about exactly what specific kind of job it is that you want. One way to finesse this situation, when asked, is to describe your overall job goal while acknowledging (try a humble smile here) that you probably will not get this kind of job the first time out. For example, suppose you have a degree in electronic engineering, and you ultimately want to design computers. You might say, "My goal is to design computers, but I know I have a few things to learn before I'm ready for that kind of job. For the moment I'll be pleased to find a training job working with people who design computers. I want to be in a position to observe and learn as much as I possibly can." This kind of response does several valuable things: It defines the kind of job you want now and in the future; it indicates your willingness to start at the bottom; and it indicates your eagerness to learn. What more can an employer ask for?

One definite no-no: When asked what kind of job you want, never say, "I don't know," "I haven't really thought much about it," or "Anything I can get." That's why you have to spend some time before the interview working out in your own mind what you really want.

What Kind of Interview Is This, Anyway?

Before you start interviewing, it helps to become familiar with the kinds of interviews you are likely to encounter during your job search. New graduates generally encounter three types: the personnel interview, the general interview, the specific interview.

The personnel interview is conducted by someone in the personnel department. It is basically a screening interview, and afterward, the interviewer will decide whether or not to pass on your name to someone who can hire you. The general, and perhaps obligatory, interview is with someone who probably does not have a job to offer and may even be seeing you only as a favor to your parents or a friend. This person is willing to talk with you, however, and if you make a good impression, you will be kept in mind for future jobs. Finally, there is the specific interview, which occurs when there is a specific job for which you may indeed be considered. Naturally, you will want most of your interviews to be of the last type.

Before you go to an interview, you should have a pretty good idea of what kind it is and plan your sales pitch accordingly. For both the personnel and the general interview, you should sell yourself as strongly as possible across the board. You cannot know what the company is looking for because there isn't a specific job, so you may not be able to mention anything specific in your background that might impress upon them how well suited you are to the job. Instead, describe your general background, mention your areas of special interest, and emphasize your overall willingness to work hard and learn as much as you can. For a specific interview, you should listen to the job qualifications (or ask about them if they are not offered), and then try to point out ways that your education or previous work experiences make you a candidate for this job.

Although you should have a pretty good idea which of the three kinds of interviews you are going into, you won't be able to predict the interviewer's technique. Most interviewers conduct either a directed or a nondirected interview. Since the interviewer knows so much more about this process than you do, it would be a nice world if all interviews with new graduates were directed, but the world is, unfortunately, not quite that nice. Lots of interviewers tend to "torture" new graduates with nondirected interviews on the theory that if one allows a young, inexperienced person to ramble about unguided, he or she will soon show his true colors. Unfortunately, that is all too often exactly what happens.

The Nondirected Interview

Signs that you have encountered a nondirected interviewer include long periods during which not much is said, and statements such as "Tell me a little bit about yourself," or "Tell me why you would like to work for this company." Nondirected interviewers often do not offer much information about the company or the job. They wait for you to ask.

When you find yourself in the midst of an interview like this, don't panic. The most helpful thing you can do is to stay calm. Be as low-key as the interviewer. You will have to work a little harder, but you can do it. When asked to talk about yourself, don't start with the day you were born. Instead, speak briefly about your education and training and any work experience you may have had. When you have finished speaking—and this is very important—*stop*. Don't say anything else. This is the one thing you can do to beat this kind of interviewer at his own game.. He is hoping you will chatter too much out of nervousness and talk yourself right out of a job, but if you refuse to do this, he will have to talk more, and you will probably find that the interview will become more directed.

If the interviewer continues to be taciturn, continue to answer his questions and then stop talking. (You can undoubtedly now see the value of all that practice you were encouraged to do earlier in this chapter.) At some point, you should ask the interviewer your questions. Ask him to describe the job or a typical day on the job or to tell you something specific about the company (this is where you can use your background data on the company).

The Directed Interview

The directed interview is, as you have probably already decided, much easier to get through. The interviewer will be livelier and will appear to take charge in a more positive sense. He will ask you specific questions or make comments that will draw you out, such as "Tell me about that paper you wrote on miniaturized transistors in compact stereos," or "I see from your résumé that you participated in a work-study program," or "What was your class standing?"

With both kinds of interviewers you are expected to answer questions with more than "yes" or "no." If your four-year class standing is not that high, this is where you point out that you made the dean's list both semesters of your senior year.

Although they are far less common now than they were ten years ago, you may occasionally encounter a "stress test" or a trick—a monkey wrench—that the interviewer throws in to see how you function under stress. The most famous stress test is to offer you a cigarette in a room where there is no ashtray. The best way to avoid that situation is not to smoke during a job interview. (In fact, a survey taken of personnel interviewers showed that most thought job seekers should refrain from smoking—and, of course, eating—during an interview.) Alternately, you may be asked to take a seat but there will not be a chair readily available.

The best way to handle a stress test is not to let it faze you. The classic and correct response to not seeing an ashtray is to say, "May I please have an ashtray?" If the only chair is a comfortable armchair placed fifteen feet away from the interviewer's desk, ask, "May I move this chair closer to you?" At this point, you have passed the test, and the interviewer will immediately spot his "mistake" and direct you to an appropriate chair or get up and get you one himself.

The Information-gathering Interview: A New Twist

As was noted in an earlier chapter, information-gathering interviews are a relatively new device developed by networkers. Unfortunately they have become an overused and even abused ploy these days, and you may find that executives are not so willing to "give you fifteen minutes of their time to talk about the field in general" as they once were. Executives (that is, those who have the power to hire and fire) are generally very busy people, and unless they have a reason to see you, such as they owe your parents a very big favor or they work with your favorite professor, you may get a relatively cold shoulder when you try to set up an information-gathering interview. You almost certainly will not get one from someone with whom you have no connection at all. There is, however, a new twist on information-gathering interviews that is perfect for new graduates: Skip the executive ranks and try instead to talk to someone in middle management or someone who has only been out of school two or three years. These people can give you the scoop on what it is really like to work for such-and-such a company. They can also give you pointers on getting through the personnel department and handling certain executives when you do have an interview, and can advise you about beginning salaries and benefits, which gives you a definite edge in the final stage of negotiations. In the long run, this kind of information-gathering interview will serve you far better than one with the very top brass.

And how do you find people like this to interview? Ask around. The career counseling office may be happy to supply you with a list of recent graduates placed in certain companies. Think about people you already know who were two or three years ahead of you in school, and find out where they went to work. Call them and ask them to give you a few minutes of their time. They will likely be flattered and delighted to help, and you will learn a lot.

When you do go on an information-gathering interview, even with someone your age, prepare yourself well for it. Have a list of questions about the company and the kind of job you are likely to get if you go to work there. Most important in this, as in any kind of interview, is to know what you are looking for so you don't waste the other person's time.

Finally, in any information-gathering interview, don't expect the person who talks with you to produce a job. The most you can expect, if you conduct yourself well, is to have made a "friend" inside the company who may be able to put in a good word for you when a job does become available.

Dressing for an Interview

How you dress for a job interview depends in large part on where you hope to work. If you have just finished law school and are hoping to land a job in a major law firm, a conservative dark suit and a white or light-colored shirt or blouse (for women), tie (for men), and dark shoes are *de rigueur*. If you want to land a job in an art department, you can afford to be less staid in your dress.

New graduates, in particular, send one of two messages with their dress. The first and better one is: "I am ready to function in an adult world." The second message, not a very good one, is: "I am not quite ready to be an adult yet, but I think you should make an exception and give me a job anyway." One new graduate with a degree in philosophy insisted on going to all his job interviews in blue jeans and a casual shirt. He told employers he didn't believe dress was important, that it had nothing to do with his ability to work well, and that he wanted to present himself in as honest a light as possible. One day, he walked into an interview as assistant professor at a very good, small college. It was a job he really wanted, despite his adamant refusal to let his dress send that message. Opposite him in the outer office was a woman, neatly if unimaginatively dressed in a plaid skirt and a blazer. Guess who got the job?

Your dress sends out a message that you have no chance to correct. An interviewer will without comment rule you out for a job if you are not appropriately dressed for an interview; he will almost never ask you why you chose to dress in a certain way. Inappropriate dress is a mistake you have no chance to recoup, let alone explain, but it's also a mistake you don't have to make.

Most new graduates, whose wardrobes are geared to their school lives, want to know if they can wear school clothes on a job interview. The answer is yes, and no, and maybe. If you're headed into a sophisticated city in search of a high-powered job as a stockbroker, lawyer, or in any other of the so-called conservative professions, then the answer is an emphatic no. You need to wear the same kind of outfit you would wear on the job—the aforementioned conservative suit is a must, in other words. For almost any other kind of job, you can wear school clothes, with some modifications. Women should try to wear an outfit or "ensemble", that is, clothes meant to be worn together. Heels and hose are necessary. Don't wear anything outlandish or low-cut. You want your mind and personality to advertise you in an interview, not your dress. Don't wear unusually expensive clothes—a fur coat or diamond earrings—or the interviewer may decide you really don't need the job. Men should always try to wear a jacket, if not a suit, and a tie. Both men and women should avoid looking either too punk or too preppy. The former looks too radical and outlandish, the latter too juvenile.

You also must pay special attention to your personal grooming. Be sure you have showered, used deodorant, and brushed your teeth. If you want to, slip a breath mint into your mouth a few minutes before you arrive at the interview. This may sound like general good hygiene, but it's important to bear in mind.

Your clothes, regardless of what you wear, must be neatly pressed and clean. Make sure there are no rips, unsewn hems, or loose or missing buttons. Your shoes should be newly reheeled, if necessary, and highly polished. Your hands must be clean, and your nails should be fairly short. (Like dressing too rich, long nails can make you look idle.) Remember, poor grooming may mean that you will be immediately disqualified for a job even though no one will ever admit to you that this is why you are out of the running.

Yes, You Have to Go Alone

While you can and will want to have a support system of friends and advisers as you job hunt, there comes a time when you must go forth alone into the world to seek your fame and fortune—and that moment is when you head out for a job interview. Never take a friend with you. Do take pens and pencils, a few copies of your résumé, notepaper, and a magazine or book to read while you wait. (The latter is not a suggestion; it is an order. If you take something to read, and then read it, you will look considerably more relaxed—even if you aren't—than if you simply sit and fidget while you wait to be called into the inner sanctum.)

Plan to arrive five to ten minutes ahead of your appointment. If you are not sure how to get where you are going, check it out a day or so in advance. There is no excuse short of a real emergency for arriving late for a job interview.

Try your best not to be too nervous, but of course, that's a tall order. The most important thing you can do to combat interview fear is to make sure everything within *your* control goes right:

- Get your clothes in order the day before or several days before the interview.
- Do your homework thoroughly so you really know something about the company.
- Make sure you have your sales pitch down pat.

- Get a good night's sleep the night before an interview.
- Eat a light breakfast or lunch.
- Leave early enough so you can arrive on time even if something goes wrong on the way.
- Remember, the company is looking for someone to hire, and *you* have a lot to offer.

8

How to Pass the Interview With Flying Colors

If you have never been through an interview, it will help to know in advance what's going to happen. And since you were just leaving home in the last chapter, let's imagine you have just arrived—ten to fifteen minutes early—at the interview. Now what happens?

Make a quick stop in the restroom (the receptionist can usually point you in the right direction) and make a last-minute check on your appearance before you officially report to the receptionist's desk. Did your hands get dirty reading the newspaper? Be sure to wash them. Is your collar neatly in place? Hair combed? You are ready to head upstairs, where the big brass is awaiting you.

Announce yourself to the receptionist and tell her with whom you have an appointment. She will probably let the interviewer know you have arrived and then ask you to take a seat. Use this time to take off your coat and any other outerwear and fold them neatly so you can easily carry them into the office with you. You will not make a good initial impression if you're scrambling to gather up your belongings when you are finally invited into the interviewer's office.

Now pull out the magazine or book you brought with you. Holding something in your hands will keep them from trembling. One word of caution: Choose something intelligent and reasonably neutral. Carrying a left-wing underground newspaper with a cover story that attacks the big oil companies when you're interviewing at one of them is not funny. Read *Time* or *Newsweek* or maybe the *Wall Street Journal.* Or read a good book, something you won't be embarrassed to describe to the interviewer if you are asked about it. Reading a technical journal may seem like a good idea, but it is actually a bit too calculated. They want a well-rounded person, remember?

Now you wait, for what will seem like an eternity to you but will probably be less than ten minutes. Eventually, the receptionist will give you the nod, or the interviewer himself will appear to escort you into the office where the interview proper begins.

An interviewer will usually greet you with an outstretched hand. If he or she doesn't, an interview is one time when you can take the initiative, but don't force a handshake on someone who obviously, for whatever reason, is not planning to shake your hand. If the interviewer remains seated or has a handful of papers and shows no signs of putting them aside to shake hands with you, then don't extend your hand. Ninety-nine times out of 100, though, you will shake hands with the interviewer when you are introduced.

As you shake hands, look the person directly in the eye. One of the marks of an insecure person is the habit of looking down when meeting another person. Don't give yourself away this early in the interview, even if you are feeling scared and insecure. Remember to keep up eye contact throughout the interview, too. You don't have to stare intensely, and there will certainly be times when you won't have eye contact. Most Americans, for example, tend to look away as they begin to answer a question. They do it automatically, and you will probably do it automatically, too. Just be careful that you are not one of those persons who *never* look anyone in the eye. Take whatever seat the interviewer directs you to. Remember what you practiced and try to sit up straight without fidgeting.

What Interviews Are All About—And What They're Not About

The interview is about to begin. But before it does, do you really know what it is all about? What its real purpose is? Most people—even some very experienced workers—do not totally understand the purpose of job interviews. Most new graduates are really lost during an interview, on top of being scared. The purpose of the job interview is to persuade the interviewer that you are the best person for a particular job. You may make some small talk while you do this; you may discuss a favorite sport that you are both crazy about or the fact that you both attended the same school; or you may even make a joke or two—but all this chitchat is extraneous to the real work of the job interview: selling someone on your skills, talents, and personality. If all goes well, the other person will start selling you right back—on the benefits of going to work for the company he represents. In fact, when this happens, you know the interview is going very well.

It is also important to understand that "selling yourself" means selling you as a viable job candidate, not as the candidate with the best looks or sense of humor. It doesn't hurt to be charming during an interview, but there are ways and there are ways of being charming. Paul, for example, waltzed through most interviews, but for some strange reason, got no job offers. He always joked with the interviewer, and all his friends knew what a good storyteller he as. Paul's great gift, in fact, was that he never forgot a good joke, and when he retold one, he always made it sound better than the last time it had been told. So why wasn't he getting job offers?

Any personnel expert could easily answer that question. Paul was too friendly, too busy showing off his congenial side. Some interviewers even invite such casual behavior from the people whom they interview. They make jokes right back. Everyone laughs and has a very good time in an interview like this. But it is a test—a particularly appropriate one for new graduates—to see how businesslike you really are. You don't go to work to socialize, although, of course, you will make friends at a job over the course of time, and if you make the mistake of socializing too much during an interview, you should not be surprised if you don't get the job.

Using your looks gets you to the same place—nowhere—on a job interview. The interviewer may be bowled over by how attractive you are and may have a wonderful time looking at you for thirty or forty minutes, but if you don't produce some evidence that there is a capable, ambitious, and intelligent person behind the good-looking face, you probably won't get the job either. It should go without saying that regardless of your sex or the interviewer's, you don't flirt.

A job interview is all about communication, from you to the interviewer and from the interviewer to you. If you fail to communicate about why you are the best person for this job and why this is the job for you, the interview will not be successful. Remember, too, that communication is the *exchange* of information. Many job experts maintain that the interviewee should do as much as 90 percent of the talking during a successful interview. Since you are inexperienced at this, and the interviewer knows it, you may get by with a little less talking, but talk you must. Be sure you do your share of communicating, and be sure you communicate about the right things.

Look out for and avoid the following signs of poor communication:

- Meandering conversations
- Failure to answer questions you are asked

- Talking too little
- Talking too much
- Failure to ask questions
- Indirectness (a failure, for example, to ask for a job description, or when the company expects to fill the job)

It is also important to realize that the smallest thing can ruin an interview: flippancy, an inappropriate joke, a limp handshake, too little eye contact, sloppy posture.

If you are like most people, you will need a few throwaway interviews to get the hang of the process. That is why it's a good idea to schedule a few interviews where you can just practice when you are beginning to look for a job.

What Employers Are Looking For

Also helpful is to go into an interview with some general idea of what employers are looking for. Above all, employers like enthusiasm and energy in prospective employees. That is why you should never acknowledge that you took the summer off and loafed at poolside when you could have been looking for a job. They also like ambition, but it must be tempered with a willingness to pay some dues, to work your way up as everyone else has done. Even if you think a job is beneath you (you really do not want and should not have to take a straight clerical job, for example), never let the interviewer know this. You have the option of saying that a job is not right for you or is not what you were looking for, but you should always do it graciously and tactfully.

Employers also like initiative. However, even if you are a new graduate with no work experience and little else to offer, don't act as if you are willing to be a slave. Never say, "I'll do anything." You won't, although you may not know it yet, and you will only find yourself in trouble if you let yourself be hired by a slave driver only to discover you really aren't the slave type, after all.

Although employers recognize that you will have to be taught how to do a job, they often look for self-starters. Will you learn the work willingly? Will you find something to do when you have not been assigned to a specific task? Will you stay late to complete an important assignment? These are all important qualities that employers value in their employees, and these are the traits an interviewer will be looking for in you. You should display these qualities every chance you get.

Employers also look for someone who can get along with others. No one willingly hires a troublemaker. Sometimes it is difficult, however, to convey to a prospective employer that you get along well with people. You can mention how much you like people, if this is a qualification for the job you are seeking, but this is suitable only for certain kinds of job interviews. If you push your love of people when you are trying to get a job working in a research library, it could be the very reason you do not get the job. Even if you cannot manage to convey your ability to get along with others, don't make the mistake of so many graduates and tip off the interviewer that you have trouble getting along with people. For example, do not tell any sour-grapes stories about ex-employers or the professor who gave you a C even though you deserved an A. It will only raise a red flag and may cost you the job.

The Most Overasked Questions

Interviews consist of questions. The interviewer asks you questions, and you ask the interviewer questions. As you progress through the numerous interviews that may be required to find a job, you will quickly realize that you are being asked the same questions over and over again. They're trite; they're clichéd; and you still must answer them in a lively manner as if they are the most important questions you will ever answer. Here are some you will hear over and over again, as well as some suggested answers. The key to responding to these questions, as you will see, is to provide upbeat, positive, and sometimes rather vague answers.

Why should I hire you? About the tenth time you hear this one, you will want to throw up your hands and say, "I don't know. Why should you?" Resist the urge to do so; instead, with a slight degree of humility, list some of your better qualities. Also describe any way in which your background makes you a good candidate for this job. You might, for example, say, "Well, I'm ambitious, and I'm very eager to learn about the electronics business. I've had some experience in sales in my summer jobs that I think will serve me well in any job I take. And I have a good, strong academic record in my science courses."

Why do you want to work for ABC Electronics? This is where you get to show off that you have done your homework. You might say something like this: "I first heard about ABC from the career counselor I'm working with. He thought it was a very exciting company, and got me excited about it. I then went to the library and found a few articles about ABC. I was most impressed with a *Fortune* magazine article that described how you had been pioneers in the field but had also, unlike many other pioneers, managed to stay one step ahead of the market's needs. I think that's why you're still on top, and that's why I would like to work for ABC."

What interests you most about this job? This question is a trap for many inexperienced interviewers. This is not where you describe what the company should be doing for you, but rather, where you state what you can do for the company. Or better yet, combine the two. Never say you are interested in a job because of the benefits or the high salary. Instead, say something like this: "I like the way the job is organized, especially the fact that I would spend several months working in different departments and learning all aspects of the business. I'm very interested in everything that goes on around me, and although I would end up working in one area, I would find it fascinating and useful, I'm sure, to have some kind of grasp of the overall workings of the firm." (Alternately, if this is not a company that operates this way, say: "I like the way your employees specialize right from the start. After four years in college, I feel I've had enough general education. I think I'm ready to buckle down and learn to do one thing very well.")

What job would you like to have in five years? This question is much more of a trap for an experienced job seeker who has to make an on-the-spot decision about whether or not to say he wants the boss's job than it is for you. It is much easier for new graduates to answer because even if you want the boss's job, there is not much chance you will get it. You could even turn this question into a bit of a joke, provided you follow the funny line with a serious answer: "Well, I know I won't be qualified for the boss's job in five years." If you know the company promotes quickly, you can add, "I would like to have worked my way up to a management position within five years." If you know the company does not promote quickly, it is better to say something like this: "I would like to have a much greater body of knowledge about electronics than I have now. And I would hope to develop and expand upon my business experience."

How long will you stay with the company? This is a trap if ever there was one, and your answer should be based to some extent on what you know about the company's attitude toward its employees. If you know the company likes to think it signs its employees on for life, then you had better sound willing to be a lifer. If, on the other hand, employees come and go fairly frequently, a more appropriate (and realistic) answer is this: "I have no time schedule for how long I will stay on my first job. I'm eager to learn as much as I possibly can and to be challenged in my work."

The next question is actually a category of questions that appear in any of the following forms:

What are your best traits? What are your worst traits? What kind of decisions are difficult for you? What kind of decisions are easy for you? The trick is to answer the question honestly; that is, if you are asked to describe a bad trait, do that. But make sure it is not a damaging bad trait, and in fact, if possible, try to make it a trait that an employer would not exactly mind an employee having. For example, say something like this: "Well, I don't really like to make any decisions quickly, and I suppose that works against me sometimes. I'm a fairly deliberate person, who needs to study all sides of an issue before deciding anything." This is actually something most employers will love to hear about you. It is also not a very specific answer, something else you should avoid in answers like this. The last thing you would ever want to do is point out a truly undesirable trait. You would never say, for example: "I'm always late everywhere I go, but I work hard when I get there." The interviewer does not really expect you to dump on yourself; he just wants to see how well you handle the question.

What are your goals? Finally, an easy one. Tell the interviewer that you want to be the very best engineer or commercial artist or account executive you can possibly be. About the only thing you should not say is that you want to be president of the company. It may be true, but after reading all the preceding answers, you should be savvy enough to know better than to admit it at your level of experience.

Playing Hardball With the Interviewer

You may come to hate the trite questions, but they are still easier than some of the really tough ones that will come your way, the ones designed to ferret out the skeletons in your closet. These are:

> Why are your grades so low?
> Why haven't you ever had a job before?
> What have you done specifically to prepare for a career?
> (usually asked of liberal arts majors)
> Why did you drop out of school junior year?
> Why did you drop out of the master's program two days before you were due to get your degree?

There's no way around it, these questions are zingers, designed to sting and possibly remove you as a top candidate for the job. But they are not necessarily questions from which you cannot redeem yourself. Most of the time, you can finesse questions like these, and depending on how well prepared you are, you can even turn them to your advantage.

For example, what if your grade point average is low? A question like this gives you a chance to explain it, whereas if you never discuss your grade point average but simply send a transcript after the interview, you might not be considered for the job because of your grades. Always try to find something positive to say. Point out that while your overall average is not as high as you would like it to be, you did make the dean's list your last two semesters, or that it is considerably higher in your major. Heaven help you if you can't come up with something like this. What were you doing wasting your time in college knowing that you would have to go out and compete in today's nasty job market? (If you are a sophomore or junior reading this book, get busy reshaping that grade point average before it's too late.)

When an interviewer requests a copy of your grades, there is nothing you can do but send them. You must give permission for a transcript to be released, but to refuse a request for a transcript will surely indicate that you are hiding something and probably hurt your chances for getting the job. Send the transcript, and if your grades are not impressive, hope for the best. Maybe the interviewer liked you so much that he won't bother reading it or won't be swayed from hiring you if he does. This is not so unrealistic a notion as it may seem, as it is a known fact that interviewers tend to hire people whom they like—those with whom they feel a bond. Many top executives admit they hire purely on instinct. Your grades may not count with certain companies as much as you might think, provided everything else about you is impressive. In fact, if your grade point average is not all that it should be, this is the one negative aspect that you might consider bringing up yourself at an interview—provided you can shed some positive light on why you have not made better grades.

You must come up with explanations to other questions similar in tone—that is, positive and upbeat explanations. To explain away the fact that you have never had a job, you might describe volunteer work you did during the summers, or note that you attended summer school—anything to make you look ambitious. As a last resort, you could say you looked for a job every summer, but could never find one. Given the rate of teenage unemployment, no interviewer should have too much difficulty with that answer. Follow up by saying that you would have welcomed some actual work experience, but you are a very hard worker and and catch up quickly once you start working. If you cannot compensate for something you haven't done, always revert to mentioning your willingness to make up for it on the job you are about to get.

Finally, when you are asked a zinger, don't look surprised. After all, you shouldn't be. If you prepared for the interview, you should have rehearsed an answer for any tough questions you anticipated you might have to deal with. Answer briefly, and try to include something upbeat about yourself. Whatever you do, don't dwell on such a question.

Illegal Questions

There are some things an interviewer cannot legally ask you. For example, he or she cannot ask:

> Your marital status
>
> Whether you have (or plan to have) children
>
> How you will care for your children while you work
>
> Any physical information (height, weight, etc., unless it is a genuine job requirement)
>
> Whether you served in the military and what kind of discharge you obtained
>
> Your age
>
> Whether you own or rent a house
>
> Whether you have a criminal record
>
> What your religious preference is

That is, an interviewer cannot ask any of these questions unless they are related to a genuine job qualification. Some interviewers either don't know or don't think they will get caught asking illegal questions, so they do so anyway. That puts you on the spot. Do you answer? If so, how do you answer?

You have several choices. You can answer, of course, and you may decide this is the smart thing to do if you really want the job—which is exactly what the interviewer is counting on. But before you do this, think about how comfortable you will be working for someone who is so interested in your childbearing or your religion or the neighborhood you live in. You can also refuse to answer such questions and point out that it is illegal, in which case you probably won't get the job because you have made the interviewer uncomfortable. Finally, you can try a middle-of-the-road approach that may or may not work (no promises here, unfortunately). You can laugh and say, "Is that a requirement for the job?" or "I'm surprised that's a relevant question. I wouldn't think it would have anything to do with the job." The interviewer may back off once he sees that you are aware of the law, and he still may hire you if you do not make him feel humiliated for having tested you by asking an inappropriate question. You might like to think twice about working for him. Weigh all the pros and cons.

Questions You Can and Must Ask

As a means of strutting your stuff, if nothing else, you must ask some questions. Even if the interviewer is very thorough and explains everything you had planned to ask, come up with at least two or three questions just to prove you're on your toes. You can also let the interviewer know you are prepared in other ways, too. If the interviewer mentions something you had planned to ask, say, "I'm glad you mentioned that. It was on my list of questions," or "I would like to ask you about that."

When the interview is closing, an interviewer may ask if you have any questions, but don't wait for this. At a lull in the interview, you should announce that you have a few questions. Here are some of the things you should find out about any job before you take it:

What is a typical day on the job like?
How long does the average employee stay with the company?

Are self-starters encouraged?

What are your chances for advancement?

What opportunities are available for you to move from one department or division to another within the company?

What happened to the person you are replacing (if you are replacing anyone)?

Don't ask at this stage about salary, benefits, or how much vacation you get. That comes later, usually at the time you are offered a job. Sometimes, these things come up in the course of an interview, especially if the interviewer is trying to impress you, but don't bring them up yourself.

Attitude is 98 Percent of Getting a Job

Studies have shown that people get hired because they are liked. If you have low grades or no work experience when some is desired, but you make a good impression on the interviewer, you may get the job anyway. The trick is to make the interviewer perceive you as someone who would be a benefit to the company. This does not mean you should go into an interview intending to become friends with the interviewer. As was noted earlier in this chapter, too much friendliness can cost you a job. Instead, you should impress the interviewer as a hard and willing worker, who is bright and eager to have this particular job. (Never mind that over the course of three days you have convinced five different interviewers with five different companies of your eagerness to work for them; that's how the game is played).

On the other end of the scale from too much friendliness, unfortunately, is too much arrogance, or any arrogance at all. Too many prospective employers are being put off by the arrogance they encounter in new graduates these days. So why do you do it? You are probably scared. Insecurity often translates into arrogance. Or maybe you really *are* self-confident. You have gotten straight A's, majored in a subject that's hot, and have graduated, to boot, from the top school in the country in your area of study. It is great to have all these points in your favor, but before you go into a job interview and ruin your chances by acting as if the company would be lucky to get you, you had better examine what you don't have on your side. You don't have a proven track record, and that is probably the single most important thing a company is looking for in an employee. And if you are arrogant, you probably don't have an ability to get along with other people. Those are two very important reasons not to display any arrogant behavior during a job interview.

And what exactly will be viewed as arrogant behavior? Reports from employers indicate that the following things are considered arrogant:

- Notetaking during an interview
- Making suggestions on how to run the company
- Stating or acting as if the job would in any way disappoint you or be beneath you
- Failing to maintain a respectful attitude toward the interviewer
- Acting as if you know or have read everything there is to know or read about the company

When It Looks as if They Want You

You will usually know whether an interview went well or bombed, but it may not be so easy to tell whether or not a company is seriously interested in hiring you. When an interviewer begins to say things like "Well, you certainly are the kind of person we've been looking for," or "I'm impressed with your attitudes (academic record, achievements, etc.)," congratulate yourself. You are probably a hot job prospect. When an interviewer compliments you this way, and you think you would like to work for this company, reply: "Thank you. I know ABC's reputation, and I would be interested in working here."

Sometimes, the interviewer will be even less subtle in approach, and may say something like "How do you think you would like living in Cincinnati?" or "When would you be available to start work?" If the interviewer starts talking salary, benefits, or, best of all, if he starts selling you on the company, you know there is interest in hiring you. You have not received a firm offer yet, though, so while you should act relatively eager to work for them, don't ask about salary or benefits at this stage, either. And while you should show healthy, eager interest, don't state outright that this is *the* job for you—not yet, anyway. Keep in mind that this is a courtship of sorts, and that you are the person being courted.

When the negotiations to hire you begin, you will want to have something to negotiate with, and the sense that you will turn down the job if the terms are not right is an important bargaining tool. Again, show interest and act eager, but do *not* say this is the only job you want. In fact, if you can do it subtly, it is not a bad idea at this stage of an interview to let the interviewer know that you are in demand. You might say: "I've been talking to several companies, but so far none has had so extensive a training program as ABC." Or: "Your training program is similar to that of XYZ Corporation." Subtle comments like this will be enough to do the trick.

When the Interview Is Ending

Before the interviewer officially ends the interview, it will wind down—especially if it has gone well. This is a vulnerable time for you as you may become nervous and talk too much. There is, in any interview, a time to stop talking. This doesn't mean you should sit silently, but it does mean that you should make only polite social conversation and should stop selling yourself. You should stop talking when:

- You have been offered a job.
- The interviewer begins to talk about himself.
- The interviewer begins to gossip about the company.

- You begin to feel the interviewer is your friend.
- You are tempted to confess to any weaknesses you have.
- The interviewer describes the job or company in a way that is designed to sell you on working there.

Whether you have been offered a job or are on the verge of being offered one, you don't want to blow everything at the last minute. And you could very well do this by confessing that you really do not feel grown up enough to have a "real job," by gossiping about the company, or by saying the wrong thing in response to a personal comment from the interviewer. Don't make this last-minute mistake after everything has gone so well.

The interviewer will signal you that the interview is ending. He will thank you for meeting with him and probably stand to shake your hand and perhaps even escort you out. Some experts think you can measure how well the interview went by how far the interviewer walks you. If you are left at his office door, it probably went well enough. If he walks you to the reception area, it went very well. And if he escorts you to the elevator, it went very well indeed.

The Second Interview

As a general rule, you will not be offered a job during a first interview. The usual scenario will be to invite you back for a second, and sometimes for several more interviews. Once you are invited back, you are probably on the road to being hired—with one notable exception, which is that some companies have a ritual, drawn-out interview process that they put everyone through. For these companies, second interviews may mean nothing at all. Fortunately, you can usually find out from a college counselor or the grapevine what the hiring process is like for any given company. That way, you will always have some idea where you are in the hiring process.

If you are invited back for a second interview, and this is not one of those companies that routinely puts applicants through a series of interviews, then the chances are fairly good that you will be offered a job. A job offer is very serious; it can change the course of your life for the next few years. Because of this, when you are offered a job, the best thing you can do is to ask for time to think it over. You may know full well that you intend to accept this job, but you still have an important step ahead of you—negotiating the terms of the job—and to do that well, you need to go away and think over the offer for a day or two. In Chapter 10, you will learn how to go about negotiating the final terms of a job.

Finding Out Where You Stand

Whether you are going through a first or second interview, there is one thing you should do near the end of the interview, and that is to try to find out what the next step is. This will also give you some reading on how the interview has gone. Especially if you are interested in a job, ask what the next step is, that is, when the company will make a decision about hiring. If you get a rather cold answer ("Don't call us; we'll call you"), you can probably lower your hopes for this particular job. If you are told exactly what the next step is ("We'll be in touch with you next week," "Why don't you give us a call in a week or so," or, best of all, "I'd like to discuss this with my boss, and I'll call you back within a day or two so we can arrange another meeting to decide where to go from here"), then the chances are fairly good that you are indeed being considered for the job. Either way, if possible, it is better to know where you stand when you leave an interview.

9

What to Do After the Interview

You will have all sorts of feelings after you finish an interview. Sometimes, the feeling you get is a real high. You think they want to hire you. They certainly acted as if they wanted you. They flattered you all over the place during the interview. Or maybe you really want the job, but you are not so sure they want you. Regardless of your feelings, figuring out what happened during an interview—call it postinterview analysis—is not all that difficult. It is also important to find out where you stand with a company after the first interview. That way, you will know whether to forget about the possibility of working there or to gear yourself up for a second interview.

Write a Thank-You Letter

If you come out of an interview with the definite impression that you would like to work for this company, there are three things you should do. First, write a letter thanking the interviewer for meeting with you. If you promised to send any extra materials, such as samples or clips of your work, enclose them with the cover letter. If possible, make it look like a package. Never cram samples into a small envelope; always send them in a big envelope that makes them look as important as they are. If you promised to have your transcript mailed to the company or to supply the names of references, be sure to mention this. A thank-you letter, by the way, is business correspondence and, as such, should be neatly typed on your business stationery. Never handwrite a thank-you letter or any other piece of business correspondence.

Keep the letter short and rather reserved. Say something along these lines:

> Thank you so much for meeting with me yesterday afternoon. I was extremely interested in everything that I learned about Computronics, and was especially impressed with your description of the training program. From what I have seen, it has to be one of the most—if not the most—comprehensive training programs in the industry. I would be interested in talking with you further about the possibility of coming to work at Computronics.

There are several important things to note about this letter. Its writer has mentioned something general and something specific that appeal to him about the company, which is a good tactic. Avoid sending a vague "I loved everything I heard about your company" type of letter. The writer of this letter also mentioned the company by name, something you should do not only in correspondence, but during any interviews. In interviews, it is a way of showing how interested you are, and in correspondence, it is proof that you have not sent the same letter to ten other companies. If you have enclosed anything, you should mention that in the letter. Write: "I've enclosed the clips of my writing that appeared in the *University Sun,* our college newspaper." Avoid formal language or business-letter jargon, which is no longer in style for business correspondence. For example, you would not want to write:

With regard to our meeting of April 22, I wish to express my profound thanks to you for meeting with me and discussing the possibility of employment with your firm at some future date. Also, please find enclosed some samples of my writing as it appeared . . .

You undoubtedly get the gist of what is wrong with this letter. It is stuffy and old-fashioned—mistakes you do not want to make at your "tender" young age.

Finally, no business letter—especially a thank-you note—should run more than one page. If you cannot say what you need to in one page, then you are probably trying to say too much. Condense, delete, smooth it out, and get it down to one page.

Contact Your Contacts

The second thing you should do after an interview that leaves you interested in a particular company is to contact your contacts. This will help prepare yourself for a second interview and an offer. You may find out where you stand. Find out as much as you can about the kind of salary and benefits package typically offered to new employees with your education and level of experience. Most important, if you have any contacts who may be able to help you get this job—to put in a good word for you, in other words—now is the time to set them in motion. Do not try to deluge the company with calls suggesting they would be fools not to hire you, but a call or two from people with impressive credentials will undoubtedly help your case at this stage.

A word of warning about using your contacts in this way: You should only gear up your contacts to fever pitch in your behalf a few times during any job search. Thus, it behooves you to analyze whether this truly is *the* job you want. If it is, then there is no doubt that you should round up all the help you can get.

Less urgent at this time but of some importance is to recontact any hot leads that are pending. This is the one time when you want to have something to negotiate with, so if some other company is interested in you, now is the time to encourage them to make an offer. Maybe you would gladly go to work for either of the companies, in which case it is wonderful to have two competitors to play off against each other. You probably cannot lose, and you will almost certainly end up with a higher salary than you would get if only one company were wooing you. And if you know that one company is your special target, you will still benefit from having another offer with which to negotiate.

Call Back

The third and final thing you must do if you are interested in a particular job is to contact the company again. Send your thank-you letter, contact your contacts, and then after about ten days (or whatever amount of time the interviewer indicated as to when the company would make a decision), call back to find out what their decision was, if they have made one, or how things stand, if they have not.

Follow-up phone calls are scary business. You may rationalize that the company should come to you, especially if they are really interested, but the world does not always work that way. Suppose they have narrowed down their candidates to you and one other person. You both interviewed extremely well. You both sent follow-up notes. You both got your transcripts there posthaste, and you both have sterling academic records. But one of you picks up the phone and asks whether or not a decision has been made. Which person looks more interested in the job? You had better believe that follow-up phone calls convey a very definite message: I'm interested, even eager, and I want to know what you have decided.

The only problem with follow-up calls is deciding how persistent to be about them. You certainly don't want to make a pest of yourself and lose the job because of that. The solution is to call back as long as you are encouraged to do so. Companies do sometimes take a long time—often several months—to make up their minds about whom to hire for a job. If they say, "We haven't decided yet. Everyone has been busy with our sales conference, so maybe you should give us another call in two weeks," that is encouragement. You should definitely call back. Whenever possible, try to pin down whomever you talk to to a time when it will be good to hear from you again. That way you will not have to sit on pins and needles wondering whether you have waited long enough between calls. If you are not given any guidance, then try to wait at least ten days to two weeks between calls. And never, ever, make a follow-up call when you have just been rejected from another job or had any other kind of disappointment and are looking for something to cheer yourself up. They will be able to hear the dejection in your voice, and you don't want that.

When You Are Not Interested in the Job

Sometimes you will leave an interview with a gut feeling that this job is not really right for you or that something went terribly wrong during the interview. Trust your feelings; something probably did go wrong, although it may not necessarily have been your fault. Some interviews are simply throwaways; nothing was going to make them go well. Perhaps you blew it (too nervous, underqualified, whatever), or maybe the interviewer blew it. Yes, you read that right: The interviewer blew it. After all, they are only human, unfortunately for you, and an interviewer can mishandle an interview so badly that he ends up not liking you (even if he would under other circumstances) or you do not like him. Maybe the interviewer had a fight with his or her spouse that morning, and in you walk—looking amazingly like that person. Maybe the interviewer had also been looking for a new job and just heard that she didn't get it, and she won't be inclined to give you the benefit of the doubt in this interview. These throwaway interviews are quite rare, actually, but you should learn to spot one when you encounter it. And don't count on anything from one. That company won't be inviting you back, most likely, but it is always better to recognize where you stand, even if the news is bad.

Employers to Avoid

Even more important than whether you get invited back after a bad interview is the issue of whether you want to go to work for certain kinds of employers. Ruling out a prospective employer is not something you decide during an interview; it is a topic for your postinterview conversations with yourself and close friends and advisers. But there are times when you will find a company or a boss unacceptable.

Here are some good reasons you might not want to work for someone or for a specific company:

- The interviewer is secretive, perhaps reflecting company policy? Your questions are brushed aside. Beware, and carefully check out any interviewer that handles you this way in an interview. Back to the library again. Are they financially solvent? Do they have a high turnover of employees? Are they a serious business or a fly-by-night operation?

- The interviewer is condescending or arrogant. Just as you have been warned several times in this book about arrogance, you also should not be treated arrogantly during an interview. If you are, handle it with quiet aplomb; this still may be a company you want to work for, as you may discover in a second interview. But this may be a company you should consider not working for.

- The interviewer undermines you. It is one thing to tell a new graduate, "We pay our trainees ten thousand dollars, but our benefits are very good," or "We don't pay high starting salaries, but we advance people quickly," but it is another thing entirely to say,

"You aren't really worth it, but I'm going to offer you ten thousand dollars." A company that starts battering your ego before they hire you won't do anything good for it after you go to work for them.

When You Get Rejected

Undoubtedly, the hardest thing about job hunting, especially if you are not old enough to have developed the toughening of the skin that comes with experience and two or three job changes, is rejection. But it happens to everyone. In fact, you may find some solace in hearing that for every 245 résumés a company receives, it invites one person to interview. Several surveys show that six to ten candidates are interviewed for every job that is filled. Right now you are probably thinking it would be easier to try for Miss America (even if you're a man), and statistically, you are probably right. These statistics are not meant to depress you, but rather to put things in perspective and to show you that you won't get a job offer every time you have an interview. And you may interview with lots of prospective employers before you get an offer for a job you want. If there is any solace in this, keep in mind that you only have to get one good offer to become a happily employed person. That's not much at all.

Occasionally, the rejection will be subtle. You will interview, and may even leave the interview thinking that everything went well. But when you make your follow-up call, you will be up against a blank wall. If the interviewer is compassionate, he or she will get on the phone when you call and tell you someone else has been hired. Or you will get a letter—too often a form letter—thanking you for your interest in the company and informing you that the position has been filled. Believe it. There has been no mistake; if you had been the person who got the job, you would have been the first to know. Sometimes you will call and call and never get through, a pretty good sign, albeit a rude one, that the company is uninterested in you.

When you are rejected personally, in person or on the phone, be as gracious as possible under the circumstances. Thank the person for seeing you. Say you are disappointed if you genuinely are, and that you hope you will be considered if there is another opening. You might even ask the interviewer for any ideas about where you might look; if you were among the final candidates, an interviewer might be pleased to give you some job leads or even put in a call or two on your behalf. (Never ask for the latter, though; always wait for it to be offered.)

If you are feeling on secure enough grounds—you liked and felt rapport with the person who interviewed you—it occasionally helps to ask why you did not get the job. This is a good reality check. You can say, "Look, I'm new at this business of interviewing. Would you mind telling me whether I did things right?" Bless the interviewer honest enough to level with you and tell you that your shoes need to be reheeled or your fingernails were dirty or you laughed too loud. Those are all things you can easily correct before the next go-round.

Most of the time, though, your failure to get the job won't be any of those things. The job may have gone to someone with a master's degree whereas you have only a bachelor's. Maybe they found someone who did not have to relocate to take the job. Maybe they hired someone who really did have better qualifications than you did. These things happen, and maybe next time you will be the candidate with the best set of qualifications.

Onward and Upward

It is important not to let rejections slow you down. There is a definite momentum to a job hunt, and you want to be sure not to lose it. Taking a week off to lick your wounds because you got one too many rejections is a good way to lose the rhythm. If anything, give yourself a reward for your efforts: go to a movie, buy yourself a record, or ask a friend to go out. But remember, a few hours or an afternoon is all you get off. Then it's back to the typewriter to compose a few more cover letters to send out with your résumé.

10

They Want You!

During the first and any subsequent interviews, you have managed to do just about everything right. You have shown off your background, displayed your academic record in its best possible light, and acted interested in and enthusiastic about the job. You have not said this is the only job in the world for you, even if you have been thinking it might be, because you want to have some strength as a negotiator if and when you are offered a job. And that day has, in fact, arrived. You have been invited back for another interview, and you are 99 percent sure this means you will be offered the job. You go to the interview, and lo and behold, they do indeed offer you the job. What comes next? Do you gleefully say, "I accept. I'm so excited. I'll be a good worker. I'll do anything you want me to do." Indeed not. Instead, you play a much cooler game than this, as you will learn in this chapter.

Saying No

You will occasionally receive an offer for a job that you know you do not want. When this happens, you still must turn down the offer graciously. Who knows, you may want to work for this company five years down the road, or the interviewer may go to work for another company and remember you well enough to want to call you up with another job offer. Whatever you do, take care not to burn your bridges behind you when you reject a job offer.

Even if you know you are not interested in a job, take some time to think about it, anyway. Tell the interviewer that you will get back to him within twenty-four or forty-eight hours. There is no reason to prolong the rejection. When you do respond, give as specific a reason as possible for your refusal. You might, for example, say, "ABC is offering me a chance to obtain hands-on experience much sooner than XYZ would," or "I feel that ABC has a more extensive training program, and that's of interest to me on my first job." If you do not have a specific reason other than the feeling that this job is not for you, you might simply say, "I really don't feel this is the job for me." Regardless of the reason you give, thank the interviewer graciously for the job offer and say that you have been impressed in all your dealings with the company. That way, you leave a door open to future possibilities.

When the Answer Is Yes

If your answer to an offer is going to be "maybe" (or a big "yes"), then you should tell the interviewer you want to take some time to think over the offer and that you will get back to him or her. Now you must spend some important time preparing to negotiate the terms of the job.

Planning a Negotiation Strategy

Do you really have anything to negotiate with? In the current job market, shouldn't you just consider yourself lucky to have found a job, and accept it with alacrity? The answer is a firm *no*. Even if you really want the job, you still need to determine the terms under which you will work. And these are very important terms that almost certainly should be subject to some negotiation.

Admittedly, you lack the negotiating clout of a more experienced, skilled worker, but you do have some very important things to offer: your potential willingness to learn, your intelligence, your education, and your eagerness to work. These qualities are important and of considerable value to anyone who employs you. They are so important, in fact, that during the negotiating process, you should never apologize for your lack of experience and skills. Here is a way of looking at the situation that will help you see what you are worth: Because you lack experience and skills, an employer can hire you for less money than a more experienced worker would be paid, but you also will undoubtedly learn the job quickly and soon become almost as valuable as an experienced worker. So while you may not be worth as much as someone who has worked for ten years, your potential is worth something, and perhaps a great deal, depending upon what field you are entering. What exactly that *something* will be is what you and the interviewer will determine during the negotiating process.

What Is a First Job Worth to You?

Before you start thinking about the specifics of the job, take some time to consider generally what a first job can and cannot do for you. When you accept a first job, you should realize that it is just this: *a first job*. You may take your first job for any number of reasons that will be different from those for any future job. For example, you may find yourself taking later jobs because they offer you status, a large salary, or a chance to live in an interesting city. A first job usually offers you none of these. It probably won't offer you much status or a large salary, and it may not necessarily offer you a chance to live anywhere exciting. It may simply provide entrée to a field in which you want to work. It should give you basic work experience, but it may just be a job in which to bide your time while you decide whether to go to graduate school or to switch fields. A first job cannot make or break your career, and you probably will not stay on your first job for more than a few years.

On the other hand a first job is very important because:

> It does provide you with experience and skills.
>
> It does teach you how to get along in the real world.
>
> It will give you a tremendous boost in self-confidence (if you choose carefully).
>
> It will help you develop contacts you will be able to use in your work and in finding future jobs.

Marilyn Moats Kennedy, author of an excellent book called *Salary Strategies*, wrote that most people follow one of three career paths during the first years of their careers:

1. Change positions every year to year and a half between the ages of twenty-two and thirty in order to boost earnings as quickly as possible.
2. Build a solid base of experience with one company, if possible, and stay with them up to age thirty, then change jobs frequently from thirty to thirty-four, with the goal of achieving a top position in one's profession by age forty-five.
3. Go to work for a large, expanding company and focus attention on climbing their corporate ladder.

You may find it helpful to choose one of these paths as a goal. Before setting such a goal, however, keep in mind that it will be tentative, and that you can—and should—shift goals as your circumstances shift.

To some extent, the goal you set will be determined by the field in which you work. If you want to join a Wall Street law firm and buck for partner, then you may plan to stay a lifetime. If you want to enter publishing, an industry where salaries are traditionally low because so many people find the field an exciting one in which to work, then you may want to job hop fairly frequently for the first ten years that you work. Sometimes, circumstances force you to change your goal unexpectedly. You may take a job with a Wall Street law firm only to discover that it doesn't provide you with an opportunity for advancement or a particularly good learning experience, so you may shift your goal and decide to get out much earlier than you thought you would when you took the job. You may join a publishing firm with the idea of staying less than two years, only to find that you have fallen into a job where you can be busy learning something every day for the next five years. You would be silly to walk away from that kind of opportunity to learn the business.

At any rate, how long you think you will stay with a job has a lot to do with the kind of salary and benefits package you will be seeking. If you only plan to stay a year or two, and you will be changing jobs frequently, you can afford to take a job that may not pay so well or offer great benefits if it does offer you a chance to learn a lot. If you think you are signing on for the long-term, then you will want to hammer out a much better employment package. As a general rule, though, and this is very important, you should always try to get the very best deal for yourself that you possibly can when you start any job.

Find Out What the Going Salary Is

Before you go into job negotiations, you should try to have some idea of what the job is worth. If you did the research suggested in Chapter 2, you may only need to review your dossiers on various companies and fields. If you did not do this, you may want to reread Chapter 2 for suggestions on how to learn what the going salary is in any given field. It would be foolish to go into any job interview without knowing what the job is worth. This is the only way you will know whether the offer you have received is low, high, or in the middle of the pay scale.

Know the Employment Package You Would Like to Have

An employment package consists of the salary and any benefits such as health and life insurance, tuition reimbursement, a credit card, professional memberships, a company car. What you hope to get and what you actually receive may be two different things, but it is a mistake to go into a negotiating session without some kind of goal. For example, your ideal package may consist of a minimum salary of $18,000, four weeks' vacation, full tuition for graduate school, full health and life insurance coverage, and a company car. You may know, however, that you will settle for a minimum of $15,000 in salary, nothing less than full tuition, partially paid health insurance, no life insurance, and the dues paid on one professional membership.

The Employer's Point of View

Employers usually know the exact value of what they are offering. This is why you will have room to negotiate. If they offer a low salary to start, they may try to balance this with a good benefits package. But they also know the salary is low, and if you are a good negotiator, they may be willing to give you a larger-than-usual starting salary. An employer also knows that if he offers a salary and benefits package way below what his competitors are offering, he will not keep his employees very long. As soon as they have gotten enough experience to move on, which usually happens after about one year, they will do exactly that. Some employers may be perfectly happy to have cheap labor and a high turnover rate, but others will be willing to negotiate a better deal if it means they can hang on to you longer. You need to figure out which kind of employer you are dealing with before you begin negotiations and then plan your strategy accordingly.

Compare Offers, If You Can

If you are lucky enough to have more than one offer at the same time, before you accept any of them or even begin negotiations, sit down and compare them. Sometimes, the benefits package that looks great at first glance because it is so inclusive may not be particularly useful to you. Benefits do add another 20 to 30 percent to your salary, but if you are single you may not need or want life insurance, so the company that offers a less complete benefits package and a slightly higher salary may actually be offering you more than the company with a great benefits package and a slightly lower salary.

Negotiations

Once you have sized everything up and weighed all the possibilities, you are ready to begin negotiating. Negotiations are a process of give and take. They are also a lot like playing tennis: You send the ball over the net, and you don't—shouldn't, actually—do anything with it until it comes back to your court. The mistake many new graduates make is not waiting for the ball to come back to their court. You should realize that not only you expect to go through this process of negotiation. Just as you have some techniques and special plays to use, so does the interviewer. That is why it helps to keep in mind the concept of a tennis game. Otherwise, you will panic and start making concessions before you need to.

Here are some hints on handling negotiations:

- After you have stated your demands, one of the simplest techniques on the interviewer's part is to greet them with silence. Don't let this scare you into talking, and possibly backing down on something you want and have asked for. Always wait until your opponent (the interviewer) reacts to what you have said after you ask for something.
- Keep in mind that you will be negotiating for salary *and* benefits, and that both are of value to you. Don't give short shrift to benefits just because you have settled on a higher salary than you had hoped for. You are only half done, and you must keep at the negotia-

tions until you have hammered out a complete package.

- When negotiating, talk specifics, and talk about one specific subject at a time. For example, if you are discussing salary, settle that before you move on. You may return to it later if you are willing to give up some of your salary for, say, a higher reimbursement of tuition, but don't link the two initially. Settle the salary and then go on to the tuition.
- Focus on your positive qualities. It is true that you lack experience and skills, but you have many other qualities that will make you a good employee, and you should be compensated for those rather than penalized for what you lack.
- Do not disagree with or contradict an interviewer when he brings up reasons that he cannot give you something you have asked for. Simply redirect the negotiations back to what you are asking for or try a new line of argument.

Negotiating Salary

When you begin negotiating salary, your goal should be to start with the top money you can get. Your future raises will be based on a percentage of your salary, so if you settle on a low starting salary, it will affect you at every step down the road.

Usually, salary negotiations open with the interviewer asking you to name your price. It is a good idea to be the first to mention a specific figure. If the employer were to mention a salary far lower than the one you had in mind, you might be tempted to lower your goal—just exactly what he would like you to do. Occasionally, with new graduates, the interviewer will mention the salary first in an attempt to make you think you must accept this salary without any negotiation. He may announce with great authority, "We pay people just starting out fifteen thousand dollars." Don't fall for this. All salaries are negotiable, and this merely gives you a figure to begin negotiations with.

If you do name a figure first, offer a range rather than a specific

number. This is also the time to make clear that you are negotiating an entire package and not just a salary. For example, you
might say: "I am looking for an employment package that offers
me compensation in the midtwenties and the usual health benefits
along with some tuition reimbursement." This can also be your
response if the interviewer has started off by naming a figure.

In this fairly simple statement, you have told the interviewer a
lot. First, you have said, "I'm not easily bluffed by your first offer
and don't necessarily plan to accept it." You have also indicated
that you are open for negotiations, and perhaps a deal can be
worked out in which you get a higher salary and less tuition reimbursement.

When negotiating salary, there are two arguments that interviewers tend to use over and over again with new graduates. Here
they are, along with suggestions for how you should respond to
them:

> *Interviewer:* If I pay you the amount you ask for, I won't be
> able to give you much in the way of compensation when you
> have your one-year review.
>
> *Your response:* I hope I'll be such a good worker that you feel
> you can reward me, but in any case I'll be willing to take my
> chances with that.
>
> *Interviewer:* If I pay you that much, I'll have to pay everyone
> who starts out the same amount.
>
> *Your response:* Does everyone in the same or similar jobs at
> ABC, Inc., get paid the same salary?

Ninety-nine percent of the time, the answer to this will be no. You
will not have to say much more; you have made your point. If it
turns out that the company does indeed have a rigid salary scale
and that individual performance is not rewarded, then you may
want to think twice about going to work for such a company.

When you are talking salary, it is especially important to keep
your mouth shut at certain times. The interviewer may assume
that you are going to be an easy mark (a logical assumption, in this
case, given the fact that you have never negotiated a salary before), so he may be surprised to get any response from you. He will

then try to use silence to frighten you into accepting his offer. Don't worry, you will probably not lose the job over this and, if anything, the interviewer will admire you for your negotiating skill. Just sit tight if the ball is in the interviewer's court. Remember, it's his turn to play, not yours.

Negotiating Benefits

Usually, you will negotiate benefits after you have settled on a salary. This is because if you cannot agree on a salary, then there will not be any benefits package to negotiate. As mentioned earlier, benefits add another 20 to 30 percent—and sometimes even more—to your income, so they must be examined carefully item by item. Benefits are generally offered as a package, but they need not be considered that way; you should examine each benefit individually with an eye to adjusting it to suit you personally. You can often trade off all or part of one benefit for another. For example, if your spouse works for a company that provides both of you with adequate health insurance coverage, you may want to trade off the health insurance in your benefits package for an extra week's vacation or for more tuition money. Many large companies fund their own health insurance programs even though they are administered by an insurance company. This means that the employer actually picks up the tab for employee medical bills, so an employer may be happy to have you insured elsewhere and may be quite willing to give you something in return for that.

When trading off benefits, be sure to weigh their value. Tuition has been mentioned repeatedly, in part because it is of interest to new graduates who may want to continue their education, but also because it is a very valuable benefit. Your money goes a lot farther when it is in the form of tax-free tuition than when the same amount is given to you in taxable salary.

Should You Accept a Job on a Trial Basis?

All jobs are probationary for the first few months. Some companies have a formal probation period and some do not, but in all jobs you are on probation until you prove yourself. The period can vary from six weeks to as much as a year. Usually, you go off probation once you have had your first job review and received good marks. If any serious criticism is offered at the review, then you should still consider yourself on probation until the next review—and, of course, you will want to change your offending behavior if possible.

Discussion of probation brings us to the issue of whether you should accept a job on a trial basis. In theory, the answer is no because the employer either wants to make a commitment to you or he doesn't, and how you are viewed as an employee will depend on how committed the employer is to you. In practice, though, if you really want a job, and have not been able to convince an employer totally that you are the person for the job, you might suggest a trial period. After all, since you are on probation in a new job anyway, there is not much difference between an official trial period and an unofficial one.

Getting Through the Probationary Period

During the probationary period, the personnel office will investigate the data on your résumé and anything you may have said during the interview. If something does not check out (if you did not go to school where you said you did or graduate with honors, for example), this will be grounds for immediate dismissal. You may even be asked to sign a statement before you are employed acknowledging that your employment is temporary pending verification of your credentials.

You also may be subject to a physical examination. More and more often today, the physical is given without advance notice and by a company physician. There are two purposes for the physical examination: to determine whether you have any physical impairment that might interfere with your ability to do your job, and to detect drug use. If even a trace of drugs is discovered in your system, it will be grounds for immediate dismissal. Unfortunately, the employer will not discriminate between a hard-core user and an occasional social user, so don't say you haven't been warned.

As for getting through the probationary period in your day-to-day activities on the job, most of what you have learned in this book about getting a job also applies to holding on to one. Here is a quick review of the basic guidelines:

- Be prompt.
- Dress appropriately.
- Project the right attitude, a combination of eagerness and enthusiasm.
- Don't expect to make friends right away, especially while you are on probation. (People will watch you for a while to see whether you are going to stay around before they decide to become your friend.)
- Ask for help when you need it. (No one expects you to know very much about your work, at least at the beginning, and asking for help will be viewed as a sign of initiative.)
- Work late or show your willingness to do so if needed. (In many fields a first job is a bit of trial by torture, the torture part being how much you are willing to sacrifice for the company. Because you lack skills and experience, employers often demand your time—as a test of your loyalty. Be willing to give it; it won't last forever.)

On a first job, you also owe it to yourself to grab every opportunity to learn something new. It will help you advance and make you more valuable in the job market—should you decide to start the whole process all over again in a year or so and look for a great second job.

11

Advice for Your First Day

Making the transition from school to a job is not easy, and you have not necessarily been prepared for it. You may even have been given the impression that there wasn't such a big gap between college and the world of real work. After all, from your freshman year on, there has been a lot of brouhaha about how you are an adult now. Don't you believe it! The adult behavior that you are expected to display in college has little or nothing to do with the kinds of responsibilities that will be expected of you on your first job. In order to make the transition easier, it helps to understand some of the differences between being a student and being an employee.

For starters, work goes on—and on. There are no semester breaks, no vacations at Christmas and Thanksgiving, and you don't get to take time off after you finish a big project. You may not even get much vacation time. Two weeks is the average, and one week is not unusual for a new employee.

There is no precise feedback such as grades. (There is some good news here in that many people find working for money a much more exciting prospect than working for grades.) Feedback is more subtle or sporadic than grades ever were. Furthermore, in college you could lie low, do your work, and often still get a good grade. At work, you have to interact. Some days you will feel loved, such as when your boss is in a great mood (for reasons that probably have nothing to do with you) or when you have done a good job on an assignment. On other days you will feel unloved, such as when your boss is in a bad mood (for reasons, again, that probably have nothing to do with you) or when you have goofed on an assignment. Don't expect a meteoric rise to fame. There will be ups and downs. Progress, especially without the measuring stick that grades provide, will seem slow and even nonexistent at times.

In many ways, work will be far less structured than school was. You are probably thinking that you did not have to report to classes if you didn't feel like it, and you do have to show up at work, and if that isn't structure in your life, what is? But the very important basic difference is that you will not always be given specific assignments. Either your work will be explained to you and you will be expected to do it without its being reassigned or even regularly checked, or you will have to ask for work to do. In other words, unlike classroom assignments, which were handed to you, you will now be expected to take some initiative. Initiative is a very important key to success in office life, so display it whenever possible. Tell your boss you have completed such-and-such an assignment, and ask what you can do next.

Excuses are less acceptable in the real world than they were at school. Professors become inured to students' reasons for not doing assignments or showing up for examinations, and so they tend to accommodate them. At work, if you are not in the right place at the right time, if you do not do what you are supposed to do when you are supposed to do it, you won't have a job long—or you won't get very far in it.

To get ahead, you need more than just "passing grades." For the past sixteen years of your life, getting a passing grade was your insurance that you could move on. To get ahead in the business world, however, you have to do better than this. Just doing your job, putting in the required number of hours every day, will not get you promotions, and it may cost your job in the long run.

If you want to advance, offer to do more than is expected of you. Again, this means taking initiative, but if you really want to get ahead, you have to let others know that this is your goal. Always be willing and eager to take on new assignments.

The First Day

This is all general advice for making the transition from school to work, but what about that first day on your first job? What is going to happen? What is expected of you?

All companies have written and unwritten rules, and one of the first things you have to do on a new job is learn both. It is pretty easy to follow the written rules. If two weeks' vacation is prescribed company policy, that's that. But if starting time is 9 A.M. but no one really starts before 9:30 A.M. (and, as is also likely, no one goes home at 5:00 P.M., either), then you will have to figure out this unwritten rule by observation.

Here are some hints on getting along from the very beginning of a new job:

- Arrive early the first day; it shows you are eager and enthusiastic. (Arrive promptly at starting time *every* day. Even if everyone else comes in later, they are not on probation and you are, so toe the line for the first few months anyway.)
- Take only the allotted time for lunch. Again, everyone else may take more, but they are not new on the job.

- Report to personnel or to the person who hired you. Don't wait in the lobby; instead, announce yourself or ask the receptionist where you should go.
- Be prepared to be left in limbo for an hour or so—or even all day. First days at work are awkward and unlike any other days on the job. You may spend part of the day filling out forms—Social Security, insurance, employment record forms—and the rest of the day twiddling your thumbs. You may be given a small assignment and then left alone when you have completed it. Gradually—almost before you know it—your days will fill up with real, meaningful work.
- Fill the time by reading everything you can get your hands on—annual reports, insurance brochures, files to which you have access.
- Clear up any questions you may have. Perhaps you do not understand something about your disability insurance policy; now is the time to check it out before you get busy with real work.
- Listen to the talk around you. Take gossip with a grain of salt, but remember the important names and try to learn the office hierarchy.
- Learn to use any office equipment you are unfamiliar with. Don't just start working on it, though, but rather, ask someone to show you how it works.
- Find out where the office supplies are kept and what you have to do to obtain what you need for your work.
- Call people (except those your age and hired at the same time as you) Mr. and Ms. until you see that everyone uses first names.
- Stay all day even if you are not doing anything. It is a ritual, and you must follow it.
- Don't be surprised if you feel some resentment or even if you feel somewhat trapped. Work is going to be difficult and challenging at times, and you will feel

tired after a good day's work. This does not mean you are not going to like your new life; you just need to get used to a new pattern of living.

- Above all, enjoy yourself. Work is a lot of fun, and it will boost your self-confidence in a way that school never could. So above all else, make sure you are getting some pleasure out of this new stage of your life.

12

Ten Red-Hot Careers

Predicting job trends is never an easy task because there are too many variables and elements that simply cannot be predetermined. The career that looks full of promise today may be overcrowded a mere four years later—in just the amount of time it takes to complete a college education and train for that career. Therefore, it would be wise to read this section on promising careers as well as to research fast-moving industries with a prophetic eye. The careers discussed on the following pages are expected to be good prospects throughout the 1980s, and you should plan to do some trend-watching on your own. To do this, read several major daily newspapers plus a couple of business papers and general magazines such as *Time, Newsweek,* and *US News and World Report*—all these publications report on job trends. Also helpful is to contact trade associations in professions that interest you; they usually have up-to-date research on job trends and openings. In addition to your own research, here is a brief discussion of ten red-hot careers.

Computer Industry

The computer industry is the obvious hot spot for careers in the 1980s, and it does promise to remain a ripe area throughout this century and even probably for the rest of our lives. Computers are here to stay, and it is inevitable that they will change our lives. In order to maintain and advance this trend, workers are needed in all facets of the computer industry. Most needed will be computer engineers (people who design the hardware), computer systems analysts (people who figure out how to use the machines), and some skilled professional executives to manage the computer companies. Least needed will be nontechnical salespeople, but humanities majors (with a little extra training) may be able to find a niche in the industry writing software. The industry is finally beginning to wake up to the fact that laypersons, not specialists, use software, and they are realizing that humanities or liberal arts majors might be the very best people to write intelligent, sensible software programs. Apart from this, the newest job in the industry, for which the demand will only grow by leaps and bounds in coming years, is the computer-security expert. The Association for Systems Management ranks the computer industry thirteenth out of 240 professions in terms of its growth potential.

Financial Services Industry

Thanks in part to computers but also to some changes in legislation, financial services is going to be a very hot career area in the next few years. The financial services industry is, in short, in the middle of a revolution. Banks and brokerage houses, which formerly did not compete with one another at all, now have become intensely competitive, and each is expanding its services and moving into the other's areas of specialization. All this means that both kinds of establishments will need larger numbers of employees to handle the new, expanding business. In particular demand will be electronics technicians (to explain the technical revolution to the managers), salespeople (to sell and service the new multifeatured accounts), and marketing specialists (to interpret the "governmentese" for everyone). In addition, with more women working, more families are earning incomes high enough to cause them to seek financial advice. The market appears to be a two-way street: the industry is growing, and the customers are multiplying.

Health Services

Health services, which grew enormously over the past two decades, has not finished expanding yet, so the demand for workers remains strong. Two major demographic changes in the population will account for continuing expansion during the 1980s in the health-services field: the population is getting older, and the elderly are living much longer than previous generations did. There will have to be an explosion of health services (and other services) to cope with this large, aging population. In particular, job experts believe that physical therapists and occupational therapists will be in great demand; a 50 percent increase in jobs for physical therapists and a 60 percent increase in jobs for occupational therapists are predicted. Also in demand will be nurses, medical technicians, hospital and clinic managers, accountants, and other office workers to staff the expanding numbers of hospitals, clinics, and social service agencies.

Telecommunications

Although the number of persons who work in mass communications is never large, there will be more opportunities than ever before during the 1980s. The powers that preside over these matters have just mandated that 140 new television stations and 125 new radio bands will be created. This means there will be jobs for technicians (technical directors, camera operators, lighting specialists, sales staff, and support staff) and creative workers (producers, directors, and scriptwriters). No, there won't be any great demand for some of the more visible and glamorous positions, such as anchors, and journalism (in the print medium, that is) is not expected to be anything other than the exceedingly tight market it has been for the past few years. It's not hard to figure out where to look for work: lots of money is being poured into cable television.

Teaching

While teaching in general is not expected to undergo any kind of revival in terms of the number of employees that will be needed, for those who want to teach there are still some areas where the demand will be greater than the supply of people to fill the jobs. If you want to find a job in teaching, train in mathematics, computer science, or adult education. Anyone with bilingual skills and a willingness to teach in urban areas will be extremely marketable. Changes in the American life-style and rapidly changing technology mean that lots of teachers will be needed to retrain senior citizens for post-retirement jobs and many workers for second careers. There will be some need for grade school teachers, but no growth is predicted in this segment of the field.

Engineering

Next to the computer industry, this is one of the fastest-growing and hottest fields for the 1980s. The only problem you may have if you decide to be an engineer is finding a school that will be able to educate you since colleges were unprepared for the sudden rise in demand for engineering graduates. The American Electronics Association stated that 197,000 jobs will be open for engineers in the next four years alone, but during that time, the colleges and universities will only graduate 87,000 persons. Competition for space in engineering schools will be intense, but the jobs will be waiting for graduates when they get out. Most in demand will be astroaeronautical engineers, electronics engineers, and med-tech engineers—and oh yes, any engineer who has coupled his/her knowledge with computer savvy.

Biotechnology

Lots of exciting research is going on in the area that might best be called human engineering, and that means that lots of research money will be going into this field over the next few years. The field is small, and you often need a Ph.D. even to get an entry-level job, but the jobs will be proliferating—mostly in research and development. Not only will demand be high for biologists and chemists but also for electronics engineers, med-tech engineers, and computer analysts.

Advertising and Public Relations

After years of negative growth potential and few jobs for new graduates, the advertising and public relations business is about to undergo a boom period that will create more than the usual number of jobs for new graduates. An MBA is an especially hot degree to help you gain entré in either field right now. Most of the jobs will be in New York, Chicago, and Los Angeles. Two elements account for the growth of this career area. First, we live in an age when many new products are being created, and second, consumers are demanding more information about new products than they ever have before. Between consumers' cries for accountability and government regulations of new products, the demand for workers to explain and promote the new products will remain strong.

Sales

Salespersons will undoubtedly be needed in selling the new products now being developed and marketed. Jobs in sales are expected to increase by 19 percent over the next decade, according to the Bureau of Labor Statistics. One million *new* sales jobs will be created in the coming decade. A new and rather interesting sales area that college graduates might want to explore is the auto industry. It is now on the rebound, and as a result of that and new technology in car manufacturing, the industry is hiring sales personnel with college educations. The National Car Dealers Association is now training college educated, technically oriented recruits from college campuses.

Consulting

The aforementioned changes in American demography and lifestyles are making consulting a new hot area in which to seek a career. Although you may think of consulting as something to do at the end of your career rather than at the beginning of it, most consultants are employed by companies and firms. Many consulting firms will be expanding, and new ones will be opening their doors over the next decade to meet demands created by an aging population, two-career families, and an increasing amount of protective legislation. Some areas to investigate are pension planning, financial planning, retirement planning, and personnel consulting in general.

OTHER READING

Dream Jobs: A Guide to Tomorrow's Top Careers, Gary Blake and Robert W. Bly, New York: Wiley, 1983. The authors discuss advertising, biotechnology, cable TV, computers, consulting, public relations, telecommunications, training and development, and travel as possible professions for the Eighties.

Real World 101: How to Get a Job, Make It Big, Do It Now, And Love It, James Calano and Jeff Salzman. Boulder, Colorado: New View Press, 1982. Second half of this book, the most interesting part, tells you how to get along on your first job.

Making the Most of Your First Job, by the staff of Catalyst. New York: Ballantine, 1981. An excellent book that deals with how you feel about it all as well as the practicalities of getting along on your first job.

Guerrilla Tactics in the Job Market, by Tom Jackson. New York: Bantam, 1978. Often gimmicky, especially for the new graduate, but some of the gimmicks really work.

90 Most Promising Careers for the 80s, by Anita Gates. New York: Monarch, 1982. This witty book is also packed with interesting ideas on career choices.

ABOUT THE
AUTHOR

Marian Faux is the author of numerous career and job guides including *The Complete Resume Guide, Clear and Simple Guide to Resume Writing, Resumes for Sales and Marketing, Resumes for Professional Nurses* (all published by Monarch Press), and *Executive Etiquette* (St. Martin's Press). She lives in New York City.